CONGREGATION FOR THE CLERGY

# DIRECTORY
# FOR THE MINISTERY
# AND THE LIFE OF PRIESTS

## NEW EDITION

© Copyright 2013 - Libreria Editrice Vaticana - 00120 Città del Vaticano
Tel. 06.698.81032 - Fax 06.698.84176

ISBN 978-88-209-9087-9

www.libreriaeditricevaticana.com

# PRESENTATION

The phenomenon of "secularisation" – the tendency to live life in a horizontal projection, setting aside or neutralising the dimension of transcendence while nonetheless accepting religious discourse – has for several decades been involving all baptized persons without exception to such a degree as to engage those, whose task it is by divine mandate to guide the Church, to take resolute positions. One of the most relevant effects of this is the departure from religious practice, with a refusal – at times conscious, and at other times induced by habitual forms of conduct insidiously imposed by a culture determined to dechristianise civil society – of the *depositum fidei* as authentically taught by the Catholic *Magisterium*, as well as the authority and role of the sacred ministers called by Christ to Himself (*Mk* 3:13-19) to cooperate in his plan of salvation and to lead men to the obedience of the faith (*Sir* 48:10; *Heb* 4:1-11; *Catechism of the Catholic Church,* n. 144 ff.).

Hence the special commitment deployed by Benedict XVI from the outset of his pontificate, at times with a revaluation of Catholic doctrine as the organic ordering of the wisdom authentically revealed by God, and which in Christ has its fulfilment, doctrine whose true value is within the grasp of the intelligence of all men (*CCC,* n. 27 ff.).

If it is true that the Church exists, lives and is perpetuated in time through the mission of evangelisation (cf. Vatican Council II, Decree *Ad Gentes*), it is nonetheless clear that the most deleterious effect on it caused by rampant secularisation is the crisis of the priestly ministry. On one hand this becomes evident in the appreciable decline in vocations and, on the other hand, in the spread of a true and concrete loss of the supernatural sense of the priestly mission; these forms of non authenticity, which in their most extreme degenerate expressions have often brought to the surface situations of grave suffering. For this reason the reflection on the future of the priesthood coincides with the future of evangelisation, and hence that of the Church itself.

3

In 1992, Blessed John Paul II, in the post-synodal Apostolic Exhortation *Pastores dabo vobis*, had already brought abundant light to shine on what we are saying, and was then the driving force behind serious consideration being given to this issue through a series of statements and initiatives.

Undoubtedly to be recalled in a particular way among the latter is the Year for Priests, 2009-2010, celebrated in such a meaningful way in connection with the 150th anniversary of the death of St. John Mary Vianney, the patron saint of parish priests and priests caring for souls.

These were the fundamental reasons why, after a lengthy series of consultations, we undertook to prepare the first edition of the *Directory for the Ministry and Life of Priests* in 1994, an instrument suited to shedding light and to be a guide in the commitment to spiritual renewal of the sacred ministers, increasingly disoriented apostles, immersed in a difficult and constantly changing world.

The fruitful experience of the Year for Priests (whose echo still resounds), the promotion of a "new evangelisation", the further and most precious indications provided by the *Magisterium* of Benedict XVI, and, unfortunately, the sorrowful wounds that have tormented the Church due to the conduct of some of its ministers, have exhorted us to consider a new edition of the *Directory* that could be more consonant with the times we are living, while nonetheless maintaining substantially unchanged the layout of the original document, as well as, naturally, the perennial teaching of the theology and spirituality of the Catholic priesthood. From the *Directory's* brief introduction its intentions are already clear: "It seemed opportune to recall those fundamental doctrinal elements that are at the centre of the identity, the spirituality and the ongoing formation of priests so they may help deepen the meaning of being a priest and heighten his exclusive relationship with Jesus Christ, Head and Shepherd: this will necessarily be to the benefit of everything a priest is and does… This *Directory* is a document for the edification and sanctification of priests in a world both secularized and indifferent in so many ways".

It would be worth the effort to consider some of those traditional themes that have been gradually overshadowed or at times openly rejected in favour of a functional vision of the priest as a "professional of sacredness", or the "political" conception that confers dignity and value on him only if he is active in social affairs. All this has often overwhelmed the most characteristic dimension, which could be defined as the "sacramental" dimension of the priest, that is to say the minister, who, while bestowing the treasures of divine grace, is the representation of Christ in his own right and, while ever remaining with the limits of a humanity wounded by sin, is a mysterious presence in the world.

First and foremost is the priest's relationship with the Triune God. The revelation of God as Father, Son and Holy Spirit is linked to the manifestation of God as Love which creates and saves. Now, if redemption is a sort of creation and an extension thereof (in fact it is called "new"), then the priest, the minister of redemption and in light of his being a source of new life, thereby becomes an instrument of the new creation. This already suffices to project the greatness of the ordained minister, independently from his capacities and his talents, his limits and his miseries. This is what led St. Francis of Assisi to write in his *Testament:* "I am determined to reverence, love and honour these and all the others as my superiors. I refuse to consider their sins, because I can see the Son of God in them and they are my superiors. I do this because in this world I cannot see the most high Son of God with my own eyes except for his most holy Body and Blood which they receive and they alone administer to others". That is the Body and Blood which regenerate humanity.

Another important point ordinarily underscored all too little, but stemming forth from which are all practical implications, is the ontological dimension of prayer, where the Liturgy of the Hours occupies a special position. Often stressed on the liturgical level is how it is a sort of prolongation of the Eucharistic sacrifice (*Ps* 49: "Those honour me who offer praise in sacrifice"), and, on the juridical level, how it is an irrevocable duty. However, in the theological view of the ordained priesthood as ontological participation in the "headship" of Christ, the prayer of the sacred minister, no matter what his moral condition may be, is to all effects and purposes the prayer of Christ, with the same dignity and the same efficacy. Moreover, with the authority the Pastors have received from the Son of God to "commit" Heaven regarding questions resolved on earth for the good of the sanctification of believers (*Mt* 18:18), it fully complies with the Lord's command to pray always, at all times and without ever losing heart (*Lk* 18:1; 21:36). It is good to insist on this point. "We know that God does not listen to sinners, but if one honours God and does his will, God will listen to him" (*Jn* 9:31). Now, who more than Christ in person honours the Father and perfectly fulfils his will? Therefore, if the priest acts *in Persona Christi* in everything he does in his participation in redemption – with the due differences; in teaching, in sanctification, in guiding the faithful to salvation – nothing in his nature as a sinner can obfuscate the power of his prayer. This obviously must not induce us to minimise the importance of the minister's upright moral conduct (just like that of any baptized person), whose measure must be the holiness of God (*Lev* 20:8; *1Pet* 1:15-16); rather it serves to highlight how salvation comes from God, how he needs priests to perpetuate it in time, and how unnecessary are complicated ascetic practices or particular forms of spiritual expression, so all men may be able to benefit from the beneficial effects of Christ's sacrifice also through the prayer of pastors chosen for them.

Stressed yet again is the importance of the priest's formation, which must be integral and without privileging one aspect to the detriment of another. In any case, the essence of Christian formation cannot be understood as a sort of "training" that touches on human spiritual faculties (intelligence and will) in what we could call their external manifestation. Formation is the transformation of the selfsame being of man, and each ontological change can only be brought about by God himself through the Holy Spirit, whose task, as we say in the Creed, is "to give life". "To form" means to give shape to something, or in our case to Someone: "We know that by turning everything to their good God cooperates with all those who love him, and all those that he has called to his purpose. They are the ones he choose specially long ago and intended to become true images of his Son" (*Rm* 8:28-29). Since the priest is, as we said above, a sort of "co-creator", his formation requires an exceptional act of abandonment to the workings of the Holy Spirit, avoiding, albeit in the enhancement of his personal talents, the danger of activism, or belief that the efficacy of his pastoral work depends on his own skills. When considered in depth, this is a point that may certainly inspire confidence in those who, in this extensively secularised world deaf to the appeals of the faith, could quite easily slip into discouragement, and from that into pastoral mediocrity and tepidity, and ultimately into questioning that mission they had so enthusiastically embraced at the outset.

Good knowledge of the human sciences (in particular of philosophy and bioethics) in order to deal head on with the challenges of laicism; the valorisation and use of the means of mass communication enhancing the efficacy of the announcement of the Word; Eucharistic spirituality as a specificity of priestly spirituality (the Eucharist is the sacrament of Christ who becomes an unconditioned and total gift of love to the Father and his brothers), and on this depends the sense of celibacy (which is opposed buy certain voices as it is badly understood); the relationship with the ecclesiastic hierarchy and priestly fraternity; love for Mary, the Mother of priests, whose role in the economy of salvation is in the forefront as an element neither decorative nor optional, but essential. These and other themes are taken up in this Directory, in a clear and complete paradigm helpful in purifying equivocal or distorted ideas about the identity and function of the minister of God in the Church and in the world. The Directory can therefore be, above all, of assistance to each priest in feeling proud to be a special member of that marvellous plan of God, which is the salvation of humankind.

MAURO Card. PIACENZA
*Prefect*

✠ CELSO MORGA IRUZUBIETA
*Titular Archbishop of Alba marittima*
*Secretary*

7

# INTRODUCTION

Benedict XVI, in his address on 12 March 2010 to the participants at the Conference organized by the Congregation for the Clergy, recalled that "the theme of priestly identity is crucial to the exercise of the ministerial priesthood, today and in the future". These words mark one of the central questions for the life of the Church, this being the comprehension of the ordained ministry.

Some years ago, drawing inspiration from the Church's rich experience regarding the ministry and the life of priests condensed in diverse documents of the Magisterium[1], and in particular the substance of the post-synodal Apostolic Exhortation *Pastores dabo vobis*[2], this Dicasterium issued the *Directory on the Ministry and Life of Priests*[3]. When published, that document responded to a fundamental requirement: "The pressing pas-

---

[1]    Cf. ECUMENICAL COUNCIL VATICAN II, Dogmatic Constitution on the Church *Lumen gentium: AAS* 57 (1965), 28; Decree on Priestly Formation *Optatam Totius: AAS* 58 (1966), 22; Decree on the Pastoral Office of Bishops *Christus Dominus: AAS* 58 (1966), 16; Decree on the Ministry and Life of Priests *Presbyterorum Ordinis: AAS* 58 (1966), 991-1024; PAUL VI, Encyclical Letter *Sacerdotalis caelibatus* (24 June 1967): *AAS* 59 (1967), 657-697; SACRED CONGREGATION FOR THE CLERGY, Circular Letter *Inter ea* (4 November 1969): *AAS* 62 (1970), 123-134; SYNOD OF BISHOPS, Document on the Ministerial *Priesthood Ultimis temporibus* (30 November 1971): *AAS* 63 (1971), 898-922; *Codex Iuris Canonici* (25 January 1983) can. 273-289; 232-264; 1008-1054; SACRED CONGREGATION FOR CATHOLIC EDUCATION, *Ratio Fundamentalis Institutiones Sacerdotalis* (19 March 1985), 101; JOHN PAUL II, Letters to all the Priests of the Church on Holy Thursday; Catechesis on Priests, in the General Audiences from 31 March to 22 September 1993.

[2]    JOHN PAUL II, Post-Synodal Apostolic Exhortation *Pastores dabo vobis* (25 March 1992): *AAS* 84 (1992), 657-804.

[3]    CONGREGATION FOR THE CLERGY, *Directory on the Ministry and the Life of Priests,* (31 March, 1994), LEV, Vatican City 1994.

toral task of the new calls for evangelisation the involvement of the entire People of God and requires new fervour, new methods and a new expression for the proclamation of and witness to the Gospel. This task demands priests who are deeply and fully immersed in the mystery of Christ and capable of embodying a new style of pastoral life"[4]. In 1994 this aforementioned *Directory* constituted a response to this need, as well as to the requests made by numerous bishops both during the Synod of 1990 and in the course of the general consultation of the Episcopate conducted by this Dicastery.

After 1994, the *Magisterium* of Blessed John Paul II abounded with material on the priesthood; a theme which Pope Benedict XVI in his turn has deepened with his numerous teachings. The Year for Priests 2009-2010 proved to be an especially propitious time for meditating on the priestly ministry and promoting an authentic spiritual renewal of priests.

Lastly, with the passage of competency over seminaries from the Congregation for Catholic Education to this Dicastery Benedict XVI wished to indicate quite clearly the indivisible bond between priestly identity and the formation of those called to the sacred ministry.

It therefore seemed necessary to prepare an updated version of the *Directory* that would include the riches of the more recent rich *Magisterium*[5]. This new version quite obviously re-

---

[4]    JOHN PAUL II, Post-Synodal Apostolic Exhortation *Pastores dabo vobis*, 18.

[5]    Cf., for example, JOHN PAUL II, Apostolic Letter issued in *Motu Proprio, Misericordia Dei* (7 April 2002): *AAS* 94 (2002), 452-459; Encyclical Letter *Ecclesia de Eucharistia* (17 April 2003): *AAS* 95 (2003), 433-475; Post-Synodal Apostolic Exhortation *Pastores gregis* (16 October 2003) *AAS* 99 (2007), 105-180; Letter to Priests (1995-2002; 2004-2005); BENEDICT XVI, Post-Synodal Apostolic Exhortation *Sacramentum caritatis* (22 February 2007) *AAS* 94 (2002), 452-459; *Message to the Participants at the XX edition of the Course for the Internal Forum, Organised by the Apostolic Penitentiary* (12 March 2009); *Insegnamenti* V/1 (2009), 374-377; *Speech to the Participants at the Plenary of the Congregation for the Clergy* (16 March 2009): *Insegnamenti* V/1 (2009), 391-394;

spects in general terms the layout of the original document, which was very well received in the Church, especially by priests themselves. Kept in mind when outlining its content were the suggestions received from the entire world episcopate, consulted expressly to that end, the outcome of the proceedings of the Plenary Congregation held in Vatican City in October 1993, and, lastly, the reflections of many theologians, canonists and experts on the matter from different parts of the world and actively present in today's pastoral situations.

In updating the *Directory* an effort was made to place the accent on the most relevant aspects of magisterial teaching on the sacred ministry developed from 1994 to our present day and time, with references to the most essential documents of Blessed John Paul II and Benedict XVI. Retained as well have been the useful indications of a practical nature for undertaking initiatives, but without entering into those details that only legitimate local practices and the real conditions of each Diocese and Episcopal Conference will be able to counsel to the wisdom and zeal of pastors.

In light of today's cultural climate it is opportune to recall that the identity of the priest as a man of God is not outmoded and never will be. It seemed opportune to recall those fundamental doctrinal elements that are at the centre of the identity, spiritual life and ongoing formation of priests so they may help deepen the meaning of being a priest and heighten his exclusive relationship with Jesus Christ, Head and Shepherd: this will necessarily be to the benefit of everything a priest is and does.

Moreover, as stated in the Introduction to the first edition

*Letter Proclaiming a Year for Priests on the Occasion of the 150th Anniversary of the "Dies natalis" of John Mary Vianney* (16 June 2009): *AAS* 101 (2009), 569-579; *Address to the Participants at the Course Organised by the Apostolic Penitentiary* (11 March 2010): *Insegnamenti* VI/1 (2010), 318-321; *Address to the Participants at the Theological Conference Organised by the Congregation for the Clergy* (12 March 2010): *AAS* 102 (2010), 240; *Vigil on the Occasion of the Conclusion of the Year for Priests* (10 June 2010): *AAS* 102 (2010), 397-406; *Letter to Seminarians* (18 October 2010): *AAS* 102 (2010), 793-798.

of the *Directory*, neither does this updated version intend to offer an exhaustive exposition on the ordained priesthood, nor is it limited to a mere repetition of what has already been authentically declared by the *Magisterium* of the Church, but rather it is intended to respond to the principal questions of a doctrinal, disciplinary and pastoral nature posed to priests by the challenges of the new evangelisation, in view of which Pope Benedict XVI saw it fit to create a special Pontifical Council[6].

Therefore, by way of example, special emphasis has been placed on the Christological dimension of the priest's identity, as well as on communion, friendship and priestly fraternity, which are considered vital goods in light of their impact on a priest's existence. The same may be said about a priest's spiritual life insofar as it is founded on the Word and the Sacraments, especially the Eucharist. Lastly, some advice is offered for suitable ongoing formation understood as a source of assistance for deepening the meaning of being a priest, and thereby joyfully and responsibly living one's vocation.

This *Directory* is a document for the edification and sanctification of priests in a world both secularlised and indifferent in so many ways. The text is mainly addressed, through the Bishops, to all the priests of the Latin Church, even if much of its content can be of benefit for priests of other Rites. The directives contained herein concern, in particular, the secular diocesan priests, although many of them, with due adaptations, should also be taken into consideration by the priest members of Institutes of Consecrated Life and Societies of Apostolic Life.

As mentioned at the outset, however, this new edition of the *Directory* represents a source of assistance for formators in seminaries and candidates for the ordained ministry. The seminary represents the moment and the place for the growth and

---

[6] Cf. BENEDICT XVI, Apostolic Letter issued *Motu Proprio, Ubicumque et semper* in which the Pontifical Council for the Promotion of the New Evangelisation was established (21 September 2010): *AAS* 102 (2010), 788-792.

maturation of the knowledge of the mystery of Christ and, with it, the awareness that while the authenticity of our love for God is gauged externally on the love we have for love for our neighbours and brethren (cf. *1Jn* 4:20-21), interiorly speaking, love for the Church is true only if it is the consequence of an intensive and exclusive bond with Christ. Reflecting on the priesthood is therefore tantamount to meditating on He for whom a person is prepared to leave everything and follow Him. (cf. *Mk* 10:17-30). In this manner the work of formation is identified in its essence with knowledge of the Son of God, which through the prophetic, priestly and kingly mission leads each person to the Father through the Spirit: "And to some, his gift was that they should be apostles; to some, prophets; to some, evangelists; to some pastors and teachers; so that the saints together make a unity in the work of service, building up the body of Christ. In this way we are all to come to unity in our faith and in our knowledge of the Son of God, until we become the perfect Man, fully mature with the fullness of Christ himself" (*Eph* 4:11-13).

It is therefore hoped that this new edition of the *Directory for the Ministry and Life of Priests* may be for each man called to participate in the priesthood of Christ, Head and Shepherd, a source of help in deepening his own vocational identity and growing in his interior life; a source of encouragement in the ministry and in carrying out his own ongoing formation, for which everyone bears primary responsibility; a point of reference for a rich and authentic apostolate for the good of the Church and the whole world.

May Mary make echo in our hearts, day after day, and especially when we prepare to celebrate the Sacrifice at the Altar, her words at the wedding in Cana of Galilee: "Do whatever he tells you" (*Jn* 2:5). We entrust ourselves to Mary, the Mother of priests, with the prayer of Pope Benedict XVI:

Mother of the Church,
we priests want to be pastors
who do not feed themselves
but rather give themselves to God for their brethren,
finding their happiness in this.

Not only with words, but with our lives,
we want to repeat humbly,
day after day,
our "here I am".
Guided by you,
we want to be Apostles
of Divine Mercy,
glad to celebrate every day
the Holy Sacrifice of the Altar
and to offer to those who request it
the sacrament of Reconciliation.
Advocate and Mediatrix of grace,
you who are fully immersed
in the one universal mediation of Christ,
invoke upon us, from God,
a heart completely renewed
that loves God with all its strength
and serves mankind as you did.
Repeat to the Lord
your efficacious word:
"They have no wine" (*Jn* 2:3),
so that the Father and the Son will send upon us
a new outpouring of
the Holy Spirit [7].

[7]     BENEDICT XVI, *Act of Entrustment and Consecration of Priests to the Immaculate Heart of Mary* (12 May 2010): *Insegnamenti* VI/1 (2010), 690-691.

# I. THE IDENTITY OF THE PRIEST

In his post-synodal Apostolic Exhortation *Pastores dabo vobis*, Blessed John Paul II depicts the identity of the priest: "In the Church and on behalf of the Church, priests are a sacramental representation of Jesus Christ – the head and shepherd – authoritatively proclaiming his word, repeating his acts of forgiveness and his offer of salvation – particularly in baptism, penance and the Eucharist, showing his loving concern to the point of a total gift of self for the flock, which they gather into unity and lead to the Father through Christ and in the Spirit"[8].

## The Priesthood as Gift

1. The entire Church participates in the priestly anointing of Christ in the Holy Spirit. In the Church, in fact, "all the faithful form a holy and royal priesthood, offer spiritual sacrifices through Jesus Christ and proclaim the greatness of Him who has called you out of darkness into his marvellous light (cf. *1Pt* 2:5.9)"[9]. In Christ, his entire Mystical Body is united to the Father through the Holy Spirit for the salvation of all men.

The Church, however, cannot pursue this mission alone: all her work intrinsically needs communion with Christ, the Head of his Body. Indissolubly united to her Lord, from Him does she continuously receive the effects of grace and truth, of guidance and support (cf. *Col* 2:19), so she may be for one and all "a sign and instrument, that is, of communion with God and of unity among all men"[10].

---

[8]    JOHN PAUL II, Post-Synodal Apostolic Exhortation, *Pastores dabo vobis*, 15.

[9]    ECUMENICAL COUNCIL VATICAN II, Decree, *Presbyterorum Ordinis*, 2.

[10]    ECUMENICAL COUNCIL VATICAN II, Dogmatic Constitution, *Lumen gentium*, 1.

The ministerial priesthood finds its reason for being in light of this vital and operative union of the Church with Christ. As a result, through this ministry the Lord continues to accomplish among his People the work which as Head of his Body belongs to him alone. Thus, the ministerial priesthood renders tangible the actual work of Christ, the Head, and bears witness to the fact that Christ has not separated Himself from his Church, but continues to give life to her through his ever-lasting priesthood. For this reason the Church considers the ministerial priesthood a *gift* given to Her through the ministry of some of her faithful.

This gift, instituted by Christ to continue his mission of salvation, was initially conferred upon the Apostles and con-tinues in the Church through the Bishops their successors, who, in their turn, transmit it in a subordinate degree to priests as co-workers of the Episcopal order; this is the reason why the latter's identity in the Church stems forth from their con-formation to the mission of the Church, which, for the priest, is realised in its turn in communion with his Bishop[11]. "The priest's vocation is thus most exalted and remains a great mystery, even to us who have received it as a gift. Our limitations and weaknesses must prompt us to live out and preserve with a deep faith this precious gift with which Christ has configured us to him, making us participators in his saving Mission"[12].

*Sacramental Roots*

2. Through the sacramental ordination conferred by the imposition of hands and the consecratory prayer of the Bishop, there is established in the presbyterate "a specific on-

---

[11]    Cf. ECUMENICAL COUNCIL VATICAN II, Decree, *Presbyterorum Ordinis*, 2.

[12]    BENEDICT XVI, *Address to the Participants at the Theological Conference Organised by the Congregation for the Clergy* (12 March 2010): *l.c.*, 242.

tological bond which unites the priest to Christ, High Priest and Good Shepherd"[13].

Thus, the identity of the priest stems from the specific participation in the Priesthood of Christ, whereby he who is ordained becomes, in the Church and for the Church, a real, living and faithful image of Christ the Priest, "a sacramental representation of Christ, Head and Shepherd"[14]. Through consecration the priest "receives a 'spiritual power' as a gift, which is participation in the authority with which Jesus Christ, through his Spirit, guides the Church"[15].

This sacramental identification with the Eternal High Priest specifically inserts the priest into the Trinitarian mystery and, through the mystery of Christ, into the ministerial communion of the Church in order to serve the People of God[16], not as an attendant to religious matters, but as Christ, "who came not to be served but to serve, and to give his life as a ransom for many" (*Mt* 20:28). It is not surprising, therefore, that "the internal principle, the virtue which animates and guides the spiritual life of the priest inasmuch as he is configured to Christ the Head and Shepherd, is pastoral charity, as a participation in Jesus Christ's own pastoral charity, a *gift* freely bestowed by the Holy Spirit and likewise a *task* and a *call* which demand a free and committed response on the part of the priest"[17].

At the same time it must not be forgotten that each priest is unique as a person, and possesses his own ways of being. Everyone is unique and irreplaceable. God does not cancel the personality of a priest; on the contrary, he wants it in its entirety, wishing to avail himself of it – grace, in fact, builds on

---

[13]   JOHN PAUL II, Post-Synodal Apostolic Exhortation, *Pastores dabo vobis*, 1.

[14]   *Ibid.*, 15.

[15]   *Ibid.*, 21; cf. ECUMENICAL COUNCIL VATICAN II, Decree, *Presbyterorum Ordinis*, 2; 12.

[16]   Cf. *ibid.*, 12.

[17]   *Ibid.*, 23.

nature – so the priest may transmit the deepest and most precious truths through its characteristics, which God respects and others must respect as well.

## 1.1. The Trinitarian Dimension

*In Communion with the Father, the Son and the Spirit*

3. Each Christian, by means of Baptism, enters into communion with God, One and Triune, who communicates His divine life to him in order to make him become adoptive son in His Only Son; therefore he is called to recognise God as Father, and through divine filiation to experience the paternal providence that never abandons its children. If this is true for each Christian it is equally true that the priest, by virtue of the consecration received with the sacrament of Holy Orders, is placed in a particular and special relationship with the Father, with the Son and with the Holy Spirit. In fact, "our identity has its ultimate source in the charity of the Father. He sent the Son, High Priest and Good Shepherd, and we are united sacramentally with the ministerial priesthood through the action of the Holy Spirit. The life and ministry of the priest are a continuation of the life and action of the same Christ. This is our identity, our true dignity, the fountain of our joy, the certainty of our life"[18].

Therefore, the identity, the ministry and the existence of the priest are essentially related with the Most Holy Trinity with a view to the priestly service to the Church and to all men.

*In the Trinitarian Dynamics of Salvation*

4. The priest, "as a visible continuation and sacramental sign of Christ in his own position before the Church and the world, as the enduring and ever-new source of salvation"[19],

---

[18]   *Ibid.*, 18; *Message of the Synod Fathers to the People of God* (28 October 1990), III: "L'Osservatore Romano", 29-30 October 1990.
[19]   *Ibid.*, 16.

finds himself inserted into the Trinitarian dynamics with a particular responsibility. His identity springs forth from the *ministerium verbi et sacramentorum*, which is in essential relationship with the mystery of salvific love of the Father (cf. *Jn* 17:6-9.24; *1Cor* 1:1; *2Cor* 1:1), with the priestly being of Christ, who personally chooses and calls his ministers to be with Him (cf. *Mk* 3:15), and with the gift of the Spirit (cf. *Jn* 20:21), who communicates to the priest the necessary force for giving life to a multitude of children of God, called together in His one People and journeying towards the Kingdom of the Father.

### Intimate Relationship with the Trinity

5. From this it is possible to perceive the essentially relational characteristic (cf. *Jn* 17:11.21)[20] of the priest's identity.

The grace and indelible character conferred with the sacramental anointing of the Holy Spirit[21] therefore place the priest in personal relationship with the Trinity since it is the wellspring of priestly being and action.

From the very outset the conciliar Decree *Presbyterorum Ordinis* underscores the fundamental relationship between the priest and the Most Holy Trinity, with distinct reference to each of the three Divine Persons: "Because it is joined with the Episcopal order, the office of priests shares in the authority by which Christ himself builds up and sanctifies and rules his Body. Hence the priesthood, while presupposing the sacraments of initiation, is nevertheless conferred by its own particular sacrament. Through that sacrament priests by the anointing of the Holy Spirit are signed with a special character and so are configured to Christ the priest in such a way that they are able to act in the person of Christ the head. [...] Therefore the object that priests strive for by their ministry

---

[20]    Cf. *ibid.*, 12.

[21]    Cf. ECUMENICAL COUNCIL OF TRENT, Sessio XXIII, *De sacramento Ordinis*: DS, 1763-1778; JOHN PAUL II, Post-Synodal Apostolic Exhortation *Pastores dabo vobis*, 11-18; *General Audience* (31 March 1993): *Insegnamenti* XVI/1, 784-797.

and life is the procuring of the glory of God the Father in Christ"[22].

Therefore, the priest must necessarily live this relationship in an intimate and personal manner, in dialogue of adoration and love with the three divine Persons, conscious that the gift has been received and has been given for the service of all.

## 1.2. The Christological Dimension

*Specific Identity*

6. The Christological dimension, like the Trinitarian dimension, springs directly from the sacrament which ontologically configures the priest to Christ the Priest, Master, Sanctifier and Pastor of his People[23]. Moreover, priests participate in the one priesthood of Christ as co-workers of the Bishops: this determination is specifically sacramental in nature and hence cannot be interpreted in merely 'organisational' terms.

Bestowed upon those faithful who, remaining in the common or baptismal priesthood, are chosen and constituted in the ministerial priesthood is an indelible participation in the one and only priesthood of Christ in the public dimension of mediation and authority regarding the sanctification, teaching and guidance of all the People of God. On one hand, the common priesthood of the faithful and the ministerial or hierarchical priesthood are necessarily ordered one for the other, because each in its own way participates in the only priesthood of Christ, and, on the other hand, they are essentially different and not only in degree.[24].

In this sense the identity of the priest is new with respect to that of all Christians, who, through Baptism, already partici-

---

[22]     ECUMENICAL COUNCIL VATICAN II, Decree, *Presbyterorum Ordinis,* 2.

[23]     Cf. ECUMENICAL COUNCIL VATICAN II, Dogmatic Constitution *Lumen gentium,* 18-31; Decree *Presbyterorum Ordinis,* 2; *C.I.C.,* can. 1008.

[24]     Cf. ECUMENICAL COUNCIL VATICAN II, Dogmatic Constitution, *Lumen gentium,* 10; Decree *Presbyterorum Ordinis,* 2.

pate as a whole in the one and only priesthood of Christ, and are called to bear witness to Him throughout the earth[25]. The specificity of the ministerial priesthood, however, is defined not on the basis of its supposed "superiority" over the common priesthood, but rather by the service it is called to carry out for all the faithful so they may adhere to the mediation and Lordship of Christ rendered visible by the exercise of the ministerial priesthood.

In this his specific Christological identity the priest must be aware that his life is a mystery totally grafted onto the mystery of Christ and of the Church in a new way, and that this engages him totally in the pastoral ministry and gives sense to his life[26]. This awareness of his identity is particularly important in today's secularised cultural context where "the priest often appears 'foreign' to the common perception. This is precisely because of the most fundamental aspects of his ministry, such as, being a man of the sacred, removed from the world to intercede on behalf of the world and being appointed to this mission by God and not by men (cf. *Heb* 5:1)"[27].

7. This awareness – founded on the ontological bond with Christ – maintains due distance from "task performance" notions that have sought to look upon the priest as nothing more than a social worker or administrator of sacred rites "at the risk of betraying Christ's Priesthood itself"[28] and reduce the life of the priest to the mere expedition of duties. All men have a natural religious yearning which distinguishes them from all other living beings and makes them seekers of God. Therefore, persons seek in the priest the man of God in whom they can

[25]    Cf. ECUMENICAL COUNCIL VATICAN II, Decree *Apostolicam actuositatem*: *AAS* 58 (1966), 3; JOHN PAUL II, Post-Synodal Apostolic Exhortation *Christifideles laici* (30 December 1988), 14: *AAS* 81 (1989), 409-413.

[26]    Cf. JOHN PAUL II, Post-Synodal Apostolic Exhortation *Pastores dabo vobis*, 13-14; *General Audience* (31 March 1993).

[27]    BENEDICT XVI, *Address to the Participants at the Theological Conference Organised by the Congregation for the Clergy* (12 March 2010).

[28]    *Ibid.*

discover His Word, His Mercy and the Bread of heaven, which "gives Life to the world" (*Jn* 6:33): "God is the only treasure which ultimately people desire to find in a priest"[29].

Insofar as aware of his identity, the priest will see exploitation, misery or oppression, the secularised and relativistic mentality that casts doubts on the fundamental truths of our faith, or so many other situations of the post modern culture as occasions for exercising his specific ministry as shepherd called to proclaim Gospel to the world. The priest is, "chosen from among men and appointed to act for men in their relations with God" (*Heb* 5:1). Before souls he announces the mystery of Christ, only in the light of which is the mystery of man understood in full[30].

## *Consecration and Mission*

8. Christ associates the Apostles to his selfsame mission. "As the Father has sent me, I also send you" (*Jn* 20:21). The missionary dimension is ontologically present in Holy Ordination itself. The priest is chosen, consecrated and sent forth to render effectively in our time this eternal mission of Christ[31], whose authentic representative and messenger he becomes. It is not a matter of a mere function of extrinsic representation, but constitutes a true instrument for the transmission of the grace of Redemption: "He who hears you, hears me; he who despises you, despises me; and he who despises me, despises him who sent me" (*Lk* 10:16).

It can therefore be said that the configuration to Christ through sacramental consecration defines the priest within the People of God, making him participate in his own way in the

---

[29]     BENEDICT XVI, *Address to the Participants at the Plenary of the Congregation for the Clergy* (16 March 2009).

[30]     Cf. ECUMENICAL COUNCIL VATICAN II, Constitution *Gaudium et spes* 22: *AAS* 58 (1966), 1042.

[31]     Cf. CONGREGATION FOR THE DOCTRINE OF THE FAITH, Declaration *Dominus Iesus* on the Oneness and Salvific Universality of Jesus Christ and of the Church (6 August 2000), 13-15: *AAS* 92 (2000), 754-756.

sanctifying, magisterial and pastoral power of Jesus Christ himself, Head and Pastor of the Church[32]. Becoming increasingly like unto Christ, the priest is – thanks to Him, and not himself – a co-worker in the salvation of his brethren: it is no longer he who lives and exists, but Christ in him (cf. *Ga* 2:20).

Acting *in Persona Christi Capitis*, the priest becomes the minister of essential salvific acts, transmits the truths necessary for salvation and feeds the People of God, leading it towards holiness[33].

Nonetheless, the conformation of the priest to Christ takes place not only through his evangelising, sacramental and pastoral endeavours. It also transpires in self-oblation and expiation, that is to say in accepting with love the sufferings and sacrifices proper to the priestly ministry[34]. The Apostle St. Paul projected this qualifying dimension of the ministry with these well known words: "It makes me happy to suffer for you, as I am suffering now, and in my own body to do what I can to make up for all that still has to be undergone by Christ for the sake of his body, the Church" (*Col* 1:24).

## 1.3. The Pneumatological Dimension

*Sacramental Character*

9. In priestly Ordination the priest has received the seal of the Holy Spirit, which has made him a man marked by the sacramental character in order to the minister of Christ and the Church forever. Assured by the promise that the Consoler will always abide with him (cf. *Jn* 14:16-17), the priest knows he will never lose the presence and the effective power of the Holy Spirit in order to be able to exercise his ministry and live pastoral charity – the source, criterion and measure of love and service – as total gift of self for the salvation of his own breth-

---

[32] Cf. JOHN PAUL II, Post-Synodal Apostolic Exhortation *Pastores dabo vobis*, 18.

[33] Cf. *ibid.*, 15.

[34] Cf. ECUMENICAL COUNCIL VATICAN II, Decree *Presbyterorum Ordinis*, 12.

ren. This charity determines in the priest the way he thinks, acts and conducts himself.

## Personal Communion with the Holy Spirit

10. It is also the Holy Spirit who by Ordination confers on the priest the prophetic task of announcing and explaining the Word of God with authority. Inserted in the communion of the Church with the entire priestly order, the priest will be guided by the Spirit of Truth whom the Father has sent through Christ, and who teaches him everything, reminding him of everything Jesus said to the Apostles. Therefore, the priest, with the help of the Holy Spirit, the study of the Word of God in the Scriptures, and in light of both Tradition and the *Magisterium*[35], discovers the richness of the Word to be proclaimed to the ecclesial community entrusted to his care.

## Invocation of the Spirit

11. The priest is anointed by the Holy Spirit. This entails not only the gift of the indelible sign conferred by anointment, but the task to ceaselessly invoke the Paraclete – the gift of the Risen Christ – without whom the ministry of the priest would be sterile. Each day the priest asks for the light of the Holy Spirit in order to imitate Christ.

Through the sacramental character and identifying his intention with that of the Church, the priest is always in communion with the Holy Spirit in the celebration of the liturgy, especially in the Eucharist and the other sacraments. In fact, it is Christ who acts on behalf of the Church through the Holy Spirit invoked in his efficacious power by the priest who celebrates *in Persona Christi*[36].

---

[35]    Cf. ECUMENICAL COUNCIL VATICAN II, Dogmatic Constitution *Dei Verbum: AAS* 58 (1966), 10; Decree *Presbyterorum Ordinis*, 4.

[36]    Cf. ECUMENICAL COUNCIL VATICAN II, Decree *Presbyterorum Ordinis* , 5; *Catechism of the Catholic Church*, 1120.

Thus, the sacramental celebration draws its efficacy from the word of Christ, who instituted it, and the power of the Spirit invoked by the Church in the epiclesis.

This is particularly evident in the Eucharistic Prayer in which the priest, invoking the power of the Holy Spirit on the bread and on the wine, pronounces the words of Jesus so that the transubstantiation of the bread into the "given" body of Christ and of the wine into the "shed" blood of Christ may take place, and rendered sacramentally present may be his one redeeming sacrifice[37].

*Strength to Guide the Community*

12. It is thus in the communion with the Holy Spirit that the priest finds the strength to guide the community entrusted to him and preserve it in the unity willed by the Lord[38]. The prayer of the priest in the Holy Spirit can be patterned on the priestly prayer of Jesus Christ (cf. *Jn* 17). Therefore, he must pray for the unity of the faithful so they may be one in order for the world to believe that the Father has sent the Son for the salvation of all.

## 1.4. The Ecclesiological Dimension

*"In" and "in the Forefront of" the Church*

13. Christ, the permanent and ever new origin of salvation, is the germinal mystery springing forth from which is the mystery of the Church, his Body and his Bride, called by her Spouse to be a sign and instrument of redemption. Through the work entrusted to the Apostles and their successors Christ continues to give life to his Church. It is in the Church that the ministry of priests finds its natural *locus* and carries out its mission.

---

[37]    Cf. BENEDICT XVI, Post-Synodal Apostolic Exhortation *Sacramentum caritatis*, 13; 48.
[38]    Cf. ECUMENICAL COUNCIL VATICAN II, Decree *Presbyterorum Ordinis*, 6.

Through the mystery of Christ, the priest, exercising his multifaceted ministry, is inserted into mystery of the Church, which "becomes aware in faith that her being comes not from herself, but from the grace of Christ in the Holy Spirit"[39]. In this sense, while the priest is *in* the Church, he is also placed *in the forefront* of it[40].

The eminent expression of this position of the priest *in* and *in the forefront* of the Church is the celebration of the Eucharist, where "the priest invites the people to raise their heart to the Lord in prayer and thanksgiving, and associates them to himself in the solemn prayer which he, in the name of the entire community, addresses to God the Father through Jesus Christ in the Holy Spirit"[41].

*Participation in the Spousal Nature of Christ*

14. The Sacrament of Orders makes the priest partake not only in the mystery of Christ the Priest, Head and Shepherd, but in some way also in the mystery of Christ, "Servant and Spouse of the Church"[42]. This is the "Body" of Him who has loved and loves to the point of giving himself for her (cf. *Eph* 5:25); who renews her and purifies her continually by means of the Word of God and the sacraments (cf. *ibid.* 5:26); who works to make her ever more beautiful (cf. *ibid.* 5:27), and lastly, who nourishes her and attends to her with care (cf. *ibid.* 5:29).

The priests – co-operators with the Episcopal Order – constitute with their Bishop a unique presbyterate[43] and in a

---

[39]   JOHN PAUL II, Post-Synodal Apostolic Exhortation *Pastores dabo vobis*, 16.

[40]   Cf. *ibid.*

[41]   *Institutio Generalis Missalis Romani* (2002), 78.

[42]   JOHN PAUL II, Post-Synodal Apostolic Exhortation *Pastores dabo vobis* , 3.

[43]   Cf. ECUMENICAL COUNCIL VATICAN II, Dogmatic Constitution *Lumen gentium* 28; Decree *Presbyterorum Ordinis*, 7; Decree *Christus Dominus*, 28;

subordinate degree participate in the only priesthood of Christ. In likeness to the Bishop they in some way participate in that spousal dimension regarding the Church, which is so well expressed with the consignment of the ring in the Rite of Episcopal Ordination[44].

The priests, who "in each local assembly of the faithful represent in a certain sense the Bishop, with whom they are associated in all trust and generosity"[45], must be faithful to the Bride and, much akin to living icons of Christ the Spouse, render fruitful the multi-form donation of Christ to his Church. Called with an absolutely gratuitous act of supernatural love, the priest loves the Church as Christ loved her, consecrating to her all his energies and offering himself with pastoral charity unto the daily oblation of his own life.

## The Universality of the Priesthood

15. The command of the Lord to go to all nations (cf. *Mt* 28:18-20) constitutes yet another modality of the priest being *in the forefront* of the Church[46]. Sent – *missus* – by the Father by means of Christ, the priest belongs "in an immediate way" to the universal Church[47], whose mission is to announce the Good News unto "the ends of the earth" (*Ac* 1:8)[48].

---

Decree *Ad gentes*, 19; JOHN PAUL II, Post-Synodal Apostolic Exhortation *Pastores dabo vobis* 17.

[44]   Cf. ECUMENICAL COUNCIL VATICAN II, Dogmatic Constitution *Lumen gentium* 28; *Pontificale romanum, Ordinatio Episcoporum, Presbyterorum et Diaconorum*, ch. I, n. 51, Ed. typica altera, 1990, 26.

[45]   ECUMENICAL COUNCIL VATICAN II, Dogmatic Constitution *Lumen gentium*, 28.

[46]   Cf. JOHN PAUL II, Post-Synodal Apostolic Exhortation *Pastores dabo vobis*, 16.

[47]   Cf. CONGREGATION FOR THE DOCTRINE OF THE FAITH, Letter on the Church as Communion, *Communionis notio* (28 May 1992), 10: *AAS* 85 (1993), 844.

[48]   Cf. JOHN PAUL II, Encyclical Letter *Redemptoris missio* (7 December 1990), 23: *AAS* 83 (1991), 269.

"The spiritual gift received by priests in Ordination prepares them for the fullest and universal mission of salvation"[49]. In fact, by virtue of the Orders and the ministry received, all priests are associated with the Episcopal Body and in hierarchical communion with it they serve the good of the entire Church according to vocation and grace[50]. The fact of incardination[51] must not enclose the priest in a restricted and particularist mentality, but rather open him to serve the one Church of Jesus Christ.

In this sense each priest receives a formation that permits him to serve the universal Church and not only become specialized in a single place or a particular task. This "formation for the universal Church" means being ready to face and deal with the most disparate of circumstances with constant readiness to serve the Church at large in an unconditional manner[52].

*The Missionary Nature of the Priest for a New Evangelisation*

16. The priest, participating in the consecration of Christ, partakes in his salvific mission according to his ultimate command: "Go, therefore, make disciples of all nations; baptise them in the name of the Father and of the Son and of the Holy Spirit, and teach them to observe all the commands I gave you" (*Mt* 28:19-20; cf. *Mk* 16:15-18; *Lk* 24:47-48; *Ac* 1:8). Missionary tension is a constituent part of the existence of the

---

[49]    ECUMENICAL COUNCIL VATICAN II, Decree *Presbyterorum Ordinis*, 10; cf. JOHN PAUL II, Post-Synodal Apostolic Exhortation *Pastores dabo vobis*, 32.

[50]    Cf. ECUMENICAL COUNCIL VATICAN II, Dogmatic Constitution *Lumen gentium*, 28; Decree *Presbyterorum Ordinis*, 7.

[51]    Cf. *C.I.C.*, can. 266, § 1.

[52]    Cf. ECUMENICAL COUNCIL VATICAN II, Dogmatic Constitution *Lumen gentium*, 23; 26; SACRED CONGREGATION FOR THE CLERGY, Directive Notes *Postquam Apostoli* (25 March 1980), 5; 14; 23: *AAS* 72 (1980), 346-347; 353-354; 360-361; TERTULLIAN, *De praescriptione*, 20, 5-9: *CCL* 1, 201-202; CONGREGATION FOR THE DOCTRINE OF THE FAITH, Letter *Communionis notio* on some aspects of the Church understood as communion, 10.

priest – who is called to become "bread broken for the life of the world" – because "the first and fundamental mission that we receive from the sacred mysteries we celebrate is that of bearing witness with our lives. The wonder we experience as the gift God has made to us is Christ gives new impulse to our lives and commits us to becoming witnesses of his love. We become witnesses when, through our actions, words and ways of being, another makes himself present"[53].

"Priests are called by virtue of the sacrament of Orders to share in concern for the mission: 'The spiritual gift that priests have received in ordination prepares them, not for any narrow and limited mission, but for the most universal and all embracing mission of salvation' […] (*Presbyterorum Ordinis*, 10). All priests must have the mind and the heart of missionaries – open to the needs of the Church and the world"[54]. This need of the life of the Church in the modern world must be felt and lived by each priest. This is why each priest is called to have a missionary spirit, that is to say a truly 'catholic' spirit, which, beginning from Christ reaches out to all so "they may be saved and reach full knowledge of the truth" (*1Tm* 2:4-6).

It is therefore important for the priest to be fully aware of this missionary reality of his priesthood and live it in total harmony with the Church, which, now just as in the past, feels the need to send her ministers to the places where more urgent is their mission, especially among the poorest[55]. Also issuing forth from this is a more equal distribution of the clergy[56]. In

---

[53]    BENEDICT XVI, Post-Synodal Apostolic Exhortation *Sacramentum caritatis*, 85.

[54]    JOHN PAUL II, Encyclical Letter *Redemptoris missio*, 67.

[55]    Cf. CONGREGATION FOR THE CLERGY, Circular Letter *The missionary identity of the Priest in the Church as an Intrinsic Dimension of the Exercise of the Tria Munera* (29 June 2010), 3.3.5, LEV, Vatican City 2011, 307.

[56]    Cf. ECUMENICAL COUNCIL VATICAN II, Dogmatic Constitution *Lumen gentium* 23; Decree *Presbyterorum Ordinis*, 10; JOHN PAUL II, Post-Synodal Apostolic Exhortation *Pastores dabo vobis* 32; SACRED CONGREGATION FOR THE CLERGY, Directive Notes *Postquam Apostoli* (25 March 1980); CONGREGATION FOR THE EVANGELISATION OF PEOPLES, *Pastoral Guide for*

this regard it must be recognized how those priests who declare their willingness to exercise their ministry in other dioceses or countries are a great gift for the both the local Church where they are sent and the local Church which sends them.

17. "There is today, however, a growing confusion which leads many to leave the missionary command of the Lord unheard and ineffective (cf. *Mt* 28:19). Often it is maintained that any attempt to convince others on religious matters is a limitation of their freedom. From this perspective, it would only be legitimate to present one's own ideas and to invite people to act according to their consciences, without aiming at their conversion to Christ and to the Catholic faith. It is enough, so they say, to help people to become more human or more faithful to their own religion; it is enough to build communities which strive for justice, freedom, peace and solidarity. Furthermore, some maintain that Christ should not be proclaimed to those who do not know him, nor should joining the Church be promoted, since it would also be possible to be saved without explicit knowledge of Christ and without formal incorporation in the Church"[57].

The Servant of God Paul VI was addressing himself to priests as well when he affirmed: "It would be useful if every Christian and every evangeliser were to pray about the following thought: men can gain salvation also in other ways, by God's mercy, even though we do not preach the Gospel to them; but as for us, can we gain salvation if through negligence or fear or shame – what Saint Paul called 'blushing for the Gospel' (cf. Rm 1:6) – or as a result of false ideas we fail to preach it? For that would be to betray the call of God, who wishes the seed to bear fruit through the voice of the ministers of the Gospel; and it will depend on us whether this grows into trees and produces its full

*Diocesan Priests of the Churches that are Dependent on the Congregation for the Evangelisation of Peoples* ( 1 October 1989), 4: *EV* 11, 1588-1590; *C.I.C.*, can. 271.

[57] CONGREGATION FOR THE DOCTRINE OF THE FAITH, *Doctrinal Note on Some Aspects of Evangelisation* (3 December 2007), 3: *AAS* 100 (2008), 491.

fruit"[58]. Therefore, never more so than today must the cleric feel himself apostolically committed to uniting all men in Christ, in his Church. "All men are called to this catholic unity which prefigures and promotes universal peace"[59].

Inadmissible, therefore, are all those opinions, which, in the name of a misunderstood respect for local cultures, tend to distort the missionary action of the Church, called as she is to carry out the one and the same universal ministry of salvation that transcends all cultures and must give live to them[60]. Universal dilation is intrinsic to the priestly ministry and therefore inalienable.

18. From the initial days of the Church the apostles obeyed the last command of the Risen Lord. Following in their footsteps, the Church down through the centuries "always evangelises and has never interrupted the journey of evangelisation"[61].

"Evangelisation, however, is undertaken differently according to the different situations in which it occurs. In its precise sense, there is the *missio ad gentes* directed to those who do not know Christ. In a wider sense, the term 'eveangelisation' is used to describe ordinary pastoral work"[62]. Evangelisation is the action of the Church proclaiming the Good News with a view to conversion, a call to the faith, a personal en-

---

[58]    PAUL VI, Post-Synodal Apostolic Exhortation *Evangelii nuntiandi* (8 December 1975), 80: *AAS* 68 (1976), 74.

[59]    ECUMENICAL COUNCIL VATICAN II, Dogmatic Constitution *Lumen gentium* 13.

[60]    Cf. CONGREGATION FOR THE EVANGELISATION OF PEOPLES, Pastoral Guide for Diocesan Priests of the Churches that are Dependent on the Congregation for the Evangelisation of Peoples: l.c., 1580-1650; JOHN PAUL II, Encyclical Letter *Redemptoris missio*, 54; 67.

[61]    J. RATZINGER, *Conference for the Jubilee of Catechists* (10 December 2000): http://www.vatican.va/roman_curia/congregations/cfaith/documents/rc_con_cfaith_doc_20001210_jubilcatechists-ratzinger_it.html.

[62]    CONGREGATION FOR THE DOCTRINE OF THE FAITH, *Doctrinal Note on Some Aspects of Evangelisation* (3 December 2007), 12: *AAS* 100 (2008), 501.

counter with Jesus, becoming his disciple in the Church, and undertaking to think like him, to judge like him, and live as he lived[63]. Evangelisation begins with the announcement of the Gospel and experiences its ultimate fulfillment in the holiness of the disciple, who, as a member of the Church, has become an evangeliser. In this sense evangelisation is the global action of the Church, "the central and unifying task of the service which the Church, and the lay faithful in her, are called to render to the human family"[64].

"The process of evangelisation, consequently, is structured in stages or 'essential moments': missionary activity directed toward non-believers and those who live in religious indifference; initial catechetical activity for those who choose the Gospel and for those who need to complete or modify their initiation; pastoral activity directed toward the Christian faithful of mature faith in the bosom of the Christian community. These moments, however, are not unique: they may be repeated, if necessary, as they give evangelical nourishment in proportion to the spiritual growth of each person or of the entire community"[65].

19. "Nonetheless, we do observe a progressive process of dechristianisation and loss of essential human values, which is cause for great concern. In the continuing evangelisation of the Church today, the large majority of the human family does not find the Gospel, that is to say the convincing response to the question: 'How am I to live?' [...]. *All men* need the Gospel; the Gospel is destined to all and not only to a specific group of people, and hence we are obliged to seek new ways to bring

[63]    Cf. CONGREGATION FOR THE CLERGY, *General Directory for Catechesis* (15 August 1997), 53: LEV, Vatican City 1997, 55-56.
[64]    JOHN PAUL II, Post-Synodal Apostolic Exhortation *Christifideles laici*, 37.
[65]    CONGREGATION FOR THE CLERGY, *Directory for Catechesis* (15 August 1997), 49.

the Gospel to all"[66]. Albeit a cause for concern, this decristiani-sation cannot lead us to harbour doubts regarding the ability of the Gospel to touch the hearts of our fellow men. "Someone may ask if the men and women of the post-modern culture, of the most advanced societies, will still be able to open them-selves to the Christian *kerigma*. The answer must be positive. The *kerigma* can be understood and embraced by any human being at any time and in any culture. In addition, even the most intellectual or simplest environments can be evangelised. We must also believe that even the so-called post-Christians can be touched anew by the person of Jesus Christ"[67].

It was Pope Paul VI who said that "the conditions of the society in which we live oblige all of us to revise methods, or seek by every means to study how we can bring to modern man the Christian message in which alone he can find the an-swer to his questions and the strength for his commitment to human solidarity"[68]. Blessed John Paul II projected the new millennium in the following terms: "Today we must coura-geously face a situation which is becoming increasingly diversi-fied and demanding, in the context of globalisation and of the consequent new and uncertain mingling of peoples and cul-tures that it characterises"[69]. What has therefore begun is a "new evangelisation", which, however, is not a "re-vangelisation"[70] because the proclamation is always the same.

---

[66]    J. RATZINGER, *Conference for the Jubilee of Catechists* (10 December 2000): http://www.vatican.va/roman_curia/congregations/cfaith/documents/rc_con_cfaith_doc_20001210_jubilcatechists-ratzinger_it.html.

[67]    CONGREGATION FOR THE CLERGY, Circular Letter *The Missionary Identity of the Priest in the Church as An Intrinsic Dimension of the Exercise of the Tria Munera* (29 June 2010), 3.3.

[68]    PAUL VI, *Address to the Sacred College of Cardinals* (22 June 1973): *AAS* 65, 1973, 383, cited in the Post-Synodal Apostolic Exhortation *Evangelii nuntiandi* (8 December 1975), 3.

[69]    JOHN PAUL II, Apostolic Letter *Novo millennio ineunte* (6 January 2001), 40: *AAS* 93 (2001), 294-295.

[70]    JOHN PAUL II, *Address to the Assembly of CELAM*, Port-au-Prince (9 March 1983): *AAS* 75 (1983), 771-779.

"The Cross stands high over the revolving world"[71]. It is new insofar as "we seek, above and beyond the never interrupted and never to be interrupted continuing evangelisation, a new evangelisation able to make itself be heard by that world which fails to find access to 'classic' evangelisation"[72].

20. The new evangelisation refers above all[73], but not exclusively[74], "to the Churches founded long ago"[75], where there are many who, although baptised in the Catholic Church, have abandoned the practice of the sacraments or even the faith"[76]. The priests have "the duty to preach the Gospel of God, following the Lord's command. 'Go into the world and preach the Gospel to every creature' (*Mk* 16:15)"[77]. They are "the ministers of Jesus Christ among the nations"[78], "owing it to everyone to communicate to them the truth of the Gospel of which the Lord has made them beneficiaries"[79], all the more so since "the number of those who do not know Christ and do not belong to the Church is constantly on the increase, and since the end of the Council has almost doubled. For this

[71]    JOHN PAUL II, *Homily of the Holy Mass in the Sanctuary of the Holy Cross of Mogila* (9 June 1979): *AAS* 71 (1979), 865.

[72]    J. RATZINGER, *Conference for the Jubilee of Catechists* (10 December 2000): *l.c.*

[73]    BENEDICT XVI, Apostolic Letter issued Motu Proprio *Ubicumque et semper* in which was established the Pontifical Council for the Promotion of the New Evangelisation, (21 September 2010): *l.c.*, 790-791.

[74]    Cf. BENEDICT XVI, Post-Synodal Apostolic Exhortation *Africae munus* (19 November 2011), LEV, Vatican City 2011, 165.

[75]    BENEDICT XVI, Apostolic Letter issued Motu Proprio *Ubicumque et semper* in which was established the Pontifical Council for the Promotion of the New Evangelisation, (21 September 2010): *l.c.*, 790-791.

[76]    ECUMENICAL COUNCIL VATICAN II, Dogmatic Constitution *Lumen gentium*, 28; cf. CONGREGATION FOR THE DOCTRINE OF THE FAITH, *Doctrinal Note on some Aspects of Evangelisation* (3 December 2007), 12; PAUL VI, Post-Synodal Apostolic Exhortation *Evangelii nuntiandi* (8 December 1975), 52.

[77]    ECUMENICAL COUNCIL VATICAN II, Decree *Presbyterorum Ordinis*, 4.

[78]    *Ibid.*, 2.

[79]    *Ibid.*, 4.

whole human race, which is loved by the Father and for whom he sent his Son, the urgency of the Church's mission is obvious"[80]. Blessed John Paul II solemnly affirmed: "I sense that the moment has come to commit all of the Church's energies to a new evangelisation and to the mission *ad gentes*. No believer in Christ, no institution of the Church can avoid this supreme duty: to proclaim Christ to all peoples"[81].

21. Priests invest and dedicate all their strength to this new evangelisation, whose characteristics were identified by Blessed John Paul II: "New in its ardour, its methods and its expressions"[82].

Firstly, "we must rekindle in ourselves the impetus of the beginnings and allow ourselves to be filled with the ardour of the apostolic preaching which followed Pentecost. We must revive in ourselves the burning conviction of Paul, who cried out: 'Woe to me if I do not preach the Gospel' (*1 Cor* 9:16)"[83]. In fact, "those who have come into genuine contact with Christ cannot keep him for themselves, they must proclaim him"[84]. In the image of the Apostles, apostolic zeal is the fruit of the overwhelming experience issuing forth from closeness with Jesus. "Mission is an issue of faith, an accurate indicator of our faith in Christ and his love for us"[85]. The Lord never ceases to send his Spirit, by whose force we must let ourselves be regenerated with a view to that "renewed missionary impulse, an expression of a new, generous openness to the gift of grace"[86]. "It is essential and indispensible for the priest to de-

---

[80]    JOHN PAUL II, Encyclical Letter *Redemptoris missio*, 3.

[81]    *Ibid.*

[82]    JOHN PAUL II, *Address to the Assembly of CELAM*, Port-au-Prince (9 March 1983): *l.c.*, 771-779.

[83]    JOHN PAUL II, Apostolic Letter *Novo millennio ineunte*, 40.

[84]    *Ibid.*

[85]    JOHN PAUL II, Encyclical Letter *Redemptoris missio*, 11.

[86]    BENEDICT XVI, Apostolic Letter issued Motu Proprio *Ubicumque et semper* in which was established the Pontifical Council for the Promotion of the New Evangelisation, (21 September 2010): *l.c.*, 790-791.

cide most conscientiously and with resolve not only to welcome and evangelise those who seek, both in the parish and
elsewhere, but "to rise and go forth", seeking, first of all, those
baptised persons who for diverse reasons do not live their belonging to the ecclesial community, and also all those who
know Jesus Christ little or not at all"[87].

Priests are to remember that they may not commit themselves only in the mission. As pastors of their people they are
to form Christian communities to evangelical witness and to
the announcement of the Good News. A "new sense of mission cannot be left to a group of 'specialists' but must involve
the responsibility of all the members of the People of God.
[…] A new apostolic outreach is needed, which will be lived as
*the everyday commitment of Christian communities and groups*"[88]. The
parish is not only the place where cathechesis is given, but also
the living environment which must actualize  the new evangelisation[89], looking upon itself as being on "permanent mission"[90]. Just like the Church herself, each community is "called
by its nature to reach out beyond itself in a movement towards
the world in order to be sign of the Emmanuel, of the Word
who became flesh, of the God with us"[91]. "In the parish the
priests will need to summon the members of the community,
consecrated persons and laypersons, to prepare them adequately and send them forth on the evangelising mission to in-
dividuals, to single families, also though home visits, and to all
the social ambits located within the parish[92]. Always remem-

---

[87]    CONGREGATION FOR THE CLERGY, Circular Letter *The Missionary
Identity of the Priest in the Church as an Intrinsic Dimension of the Exercise of the Tria
Munera* (29 June 2010), 3.3.1.

[88]    JOHN PAUL II, Apostolic Letter *Novo millennio ineunte*, 40.

[89]    Cf. JOHN PAUL II, *Homily of the Holy Mass in the Sanctuary of the Holy
Cross of Mogila* (9 June 1979), *l.c.*

[90]    CONGREGATION FOR THE CLERGY, Circular Letter *The Missionary
Identity of the Priest in the Church as an Intrinsic Dimension of the Exercise of the Tria
Munera* (29 June 2010),  Conclusion: *l.c.*, 36.

[91]    *Ibid.*, 11.

[92]    *Ibid.*, 28.

bering that the Church is "mystery of communion and mission"[93], pastors will bring their communities to be witnesses with their "faith that is professed, celebrated, lived and prayed"[94], and with their enthusiasm[95]. Pope Paul VI exhorted people to joy: "May the world of our time, which is searching, sometimes with anguish, sometimes with hope, be enabled to receive the Good News not from evangelisers who are dejected, discouraged, impatient or anxious, but from ministers of the Gospel whose lives glow with fervour, who have first received themselves the joy of Christ [...]"[96]. The faithful need to be encouraged by their pastors so they will not fear announcing the faith in a frank manner, all the more so when those who evangelise experience this missionary endeavour as a source of personal renewal: "Missionary activity renews the Church, revitalizes faith and Christian identity, and offers fresh enthusiasm and new incentive. *Faith is strengthened when it is given to others*"[97].

22. Evangelisation is also new in its methods. Motivated by the Apostle who exclaimed: "Woe to me if I did not preach the Gospel" (*1Cor* 9:16), it will be able to avail itself of all those means of transmission offered to it by the sciences and modern technology[98].

Everything certainly does not depend on such means or on human abilities, since divine grace can exercise its effect independently from the workings of man; in the plan of God,

93    JOHN PAUL II, Post-Synodal Apostolic Exhortation *Pastores gregis* (16 October 2003), 37.
94    BENEDICT XVI, Apostolic Letter issued Motu Proprio *Porta fidei* (11 October 2011), 9: *AAS* 103 (2011), 728.
95    Cf. BENEDICT XVI, Post-Synodal Apostolic Exhortation *Africae munus* (19 November 2011): *l.c.*, 171.
96    PAUL VI, Post-Synodal Apostolic Exhortation *Evangelii nuntiandi* (8 December 1975), 80.
97    JOHN PAUL II, Encyclical Letter *Redemptoris missio*, 2.
98    Cf. BENEDICT XVI, Post-Synodal Apostolic Exhortation *Africae munus* (19 November 2011): *l.c.*, 171.

however, the preaching of the Word is customarily the privileged channel for the transmission of the faith and for the evangelising mission.

He will also be able to involve laypersons in evangelisation via these modern means of communication. In any case, his participation in these new ambits will always have to reflect special charity, supernatural sense, moderation and temperance in order to see to it that people feel attracted not to the priest himself, but rather to the Person of Jesus Christ, our Lord.

23. The third characteristic of the new evangelisation is the newness of its expression. In a changing world the awareness of one's mission as an announcer of the Gospel, insofar as an instrument of Christ and the Holy Spirit, will have to become increasingly concrete in pastoral terms so the priest, in the light of the Word of God, may give life to situations and environments in which he exercises his ministry.

In order to be efficacious and credible it is therefore important for the priest – from the outlook of the faith and his ministry, and with due constructive critical sense – to be familiar with the ideologies, language, cultural interweavings and typologies circulated through the means of communication, and which to a great extent condition people's frames of mind. He will be able to address himself to one and all "without ever hiding the most radical demands of the Gospel message, but taking into account each person's needs in regard to their sensitivity and language, after the example of St. Paul who declared: 'I have become all things to all men, that I might by all means save some' (*1Cor* 9:22)"[99]. The Second Vatican Ecumenical Council affirmed that the Church "learned early in its history to express the Christian message in the concepts and language of different peoples and tried to clarify it in the light of the wisdom of their philosophers; it was an attempt to adapt the Gospel to the understanding of all men and the requirments of the learned, insofar as this could be done. Indeed,

---

[99]     JOHN PAUL II, Apostolic Letter *Novo millennio ineunte*, 40.

this kind of adaptation and preaching of the revealed Word must ever be the law of all evangelisation"[100]. In full respect for the ever diversified journey of each person and with due attention for the diverse cultures into which the Christian message is to be brought, while remaining completely true to itself and with unswerving fidelity to the proclamation of the Gospel and the tradition of the Church, Christianity of the third millennium will thereby also bear the faces of many ancient and modern cultures, whose specific values are not denied, but purified and brought to their fullness[101].

*Spiritual Fatherhood*

24. The pastoral vocation of priests is both great and universal: it is directed towards the whole Church and is also missionary. "Normally, it is linked to the service of a particular community of the People of God, in which each individual expects attention, care and love"[102]. The ministry of the priest is therefore also the ministry of fatherhood[103]. Through his dedication to souls many are those generated to the new life in Christ. This is a true spiritual fatherhood as St. Paul exclaimed: "You might have thousands of guardians in Christ, but not more than one father and it was I who begot you in Christ Jesus by preaching the Good News" (*1Cor* 4:15).

Just like Abraham, the priest becomes "father of many nations" (*Rm* 4:18), and in the Christian growth flourishing around him discovers the reward for the toils and sufferings of his daily service. Moreover, on the supernatural level as well as the natural level, the mission of fatherhood ends not with birth, but extends to and embraces all life long: "Who welcomed your soul at the beginning of your life? The priest.

---

[100]   ECUMENICAL COUNCIL VATICAN II, Constitution *Gaudium et spes*, 44.

[101]   Cf. JOHN PAUL II, Apostolic Letter *Novo millennio ineunte*, 40.

[102]   JOHN PAUL II, *Letter to Priests on Holy Thursday* (8 April 1979), 8: *AAS* 71 (1979), 393-417.

[103]   Cf. ECUMENICAL COUNCIL VATICAN II, Decree *Presbyterorum Ordinis*, 16; PAUL VI, Encyclical Letter *Sacerdotalis caelibatus*, 56.

Who feeds your soul and gives it strength for its journey? The priest. Who will prepare it to appear before God, bathing it one last time in the blood of Jesus Christ? The priest, always the priest. And if this soul should happen to die [as a result of sin], who will raise it up, who will restore its calm and peace? Again, the priest... After God, the priest is everything!... Only in heaven will he fully realize what he is"[104].

Priests make of their life those vibrant words of the Apostle: "My children, I must go through the pain of giving birth to you all over again, until Christ is formed in you" (*Gal* 4:19). Thus with generosity renewed each day do they live this gift of spiritual fatherhood and orient to it the fulfilment of each task of their ministry.

*Authority as "amoris officium"*

25. Another sign of the fact that the priest *is in the forefront* of the Church is his being a guide who leads to sanctification the faithful entrusted to his ministry, which is essentially pastoral, presenting himself, however, with that authoritativeness which captivates and renders the message credible (cf. *Mt* 7:29). Indeed, all authority is exercised in a spirit of service as *amoris officium* and unpretentious dedication for the good of the flock (cf. *Jn* 10:11; 13:14)[105].

This reality to be lived with humility and coherence can be subject to two opposite temptations. The first is that of carrying out the ministry in an overbearing manner (cf. *Lk* 22:24-27; *1Pt* 5:1-4); while the second temptation is that of disdaining personal configuration to Christ, Head and Shepherd, because of an incorrect view of community.

The first temptation was also strong for the selfsame dis-

---

[104] ST. JOHN MARY VIANNEY, in B. NODET, *Le curé d'Ars. Sa pensée - Son cœur*, éd. Xavier Mappus, Foi Vivante, 1966, 98-99 (quoted in BENEDICT XVI, *Letter Proclaiming a Year for Priests on the Occasion of the 150th Anniversary of the "Dies natalis" of John Mary Vianney* (16 June 2009): *l.c.*, 1009.

[105] Cf ST. AUGUSTINE, *In Iohannis Evangelium Tractatus*, 123, 5: *CCL* 36, 678; ECUMENICAL COUNCIL VATICAN II, Decree *Presbyterorum Ordinis*, 14.

ciples and was corrected promptly and repeatedly by Jesus Himself. When this dimension wanes it isn't difficult to succumb to the temptation of 'clericalism' with a desire to lord it over the laity, and this always generates antagonism between the sacred ministers and the people.

The priest must not see his role reduced to a mere management position. He is the mediator, the bridge, he who is always to remember that the Lord and Master, "came not to be served, but to serve" (*Mk* 10:45); bent down to wash the feet of his disciples (cf. *Jn* 13:5) before dying on the Cross and before sending them out to the whole world (cf. *Jn* 20:21). Thus the priest, ever attentive to the care of the flock belonging to the Lord, will strive "protect his flock, to feed it and to lead it to him, the true Good Shepherd, who wishes the salvation of all. Feeding the Lord's flock, therefore, is a ministry of vigilant love that demands our total dedication, to the last drop of energy and, if necessary, the sacrifice of our lives"[106].

Priests will bear authentic witness to the Risen Lord, given to whom was "all power in heaven and on earth" (*Mt* 28:18), if they exercise it in humble yet authoritative service to their respective flock[107] and with respect to the duties which Christ and the Church entrust to the lay faithful[108] and to the faithful consecrated by virtue of the profession of the evangelical counsels[109].

*The Temptation of Democratism and Equalitarianism*

26. On occasions it happens that, in order to avoid this first deviation, people fall into the second one, which tends to eliminate any difference of roles among the members of the Body of Christ, which is the Church, negating in practice the distinction

---

[106]   BENEDICT XVI, *Address to the Members of the XI Ordinary Council of the General Secretariat of the Synod of Bishops* (1 June 2006): *Insegnamenti* II/1 (2006), 746-748.

[107]   Cf. JOHN PAUL II, Post-Synodal Apostolic Exhortation *Pastores dabo vobis*, 21; *C.I.C.*, can. 274.

[108]   Cf. *C.I.C.*, cann. 275, § 2; 529, § 1.

[109]   Cf. *ibid.*, can. 574, § 1.

between the common or baptismal priesthood and the ministerial priesthood[110].

Evident at present among the diverse forms of this negation is what is called "democratism", which leads to non recognition of the authority and capital grace of Christ present in the sacred ministers and to distort the Church as the Mystical Body of Christ. It should be recalled in this regard that the Church recognises all the merits and goods that the democratic culture has brought to human society. Moreover, it fields all the means at its disposal in the battle for the recognition of the equal dignity of all persons. On the basis of Revelation, the Second Vatican Ecumenical Council spoke quite openly about the common dignity of all those baptised in the Church[111]. Nonetheless, it is necessary to affirm that the ultimate foundation of both this radical equality and the diversity of conditions and tasks is the selfsame nature of the Church.

The Church, indeed, owes its existence and structure to the salvific plan of God and contemplates herself as a *gift* of the benevolence of a Father, who has saved her through the humiliation of his Son on the cross. Therefore, the Church, through the Holy Spirit, wishes to be completely conformed and faithful to the free and liberating will of her Lord Jesus Christ. This mystery of salvation makes the Church by its specific nature a reality diverse from human society.

Therefore, inadmissible in the Church is a certain mentality, evident at times especially in some organs of ecclesial participation, and which tends to confuse the duties of priests with those of the lay faithful, fails to distinguish the authority

---

[110] Cf. ECUMENICAL COUNCIL OF TRENT, Sessio XXIII, *De Sacramento Ordinis*, cap. 1 and 4, cann. 3, 4, 6: *DS* 1763-1776; ECUMENICAL COUNCIL VATICAN II, Dogmatic Constitution *Lumen gentium* 10; SACRED CONGREGATION FOR THE DOCTRINE OF THE FAITH, Letter to the Bishops of the Catholic Church on Certain Questions Concerning the Minister of the Eucharist *Sacerdotium ministeriale* (6 August 1983), 1: *AAS* 75 (1983), 1001.

[111] Cf. ECUMENICAL COUNCIL VATICAN II, Dogmatic Constitution *Lumen gentium*, 9, 32; *C.I.C.*, can. 208.

proper to the Bishop from that of priests as collaborators of Bishops, and no longer heeds the universal *Magisterium* exercised by the Roman Pontiff in his primatial function willed by the Lord. In many ways it is a matter of an attempt to transfer automatically to the Church the mentality and praxis existent in some socio-political and cultural currents of our time without taking into due account the fact that the Church owes its existence and structure to the salvific design of God in Christ.

It must be recalled in this regard that neither the presbytery nor the council of priests — the legal institute augured by the decree *Presbyterorum Ordinis*[112] — are expressions of the right of association of clerics, and even less so can they be understood akin to a labour union pursuing claims and partisan interests alien to ecclesial communion[113].

*The Distinction between the Common Priesthood and the Ministerial Priesthood*

27. The distinction between the common or baptismal priesthood and the ministerial priesthood, far from creating separation or division among the members of the Christian community, harmonises and unifies the life of the Church, because "though they differ essentially and not only in degree, the common priesthood of the faithful and the ministerial or hierarchical priesthood are none the less ordered to one another"[114]. Indeed, insofar as the Body of Christ, the Church is an organic communion among all the members, in which each one serves the life of the whole by fulfilling his own distinct role and specific vocation (*1 Cor* 12:12 ff.)[115].

---

[112] Cf. ECUMENICAL COUNCIL VATICAN II, Decree *Presbyterorum Ordinis*, 7.

[113] Cf. *ibid.*

[114] ECUMENICAL COUNCIL VATICAN II, Dogmatic Constitution *Lumen gentium*, 10.

[115] Cf. CONGREGATION FOR THE EVANGELISATION OF PEOPLES, *Pastoral Guide for The Diocesan Priests of the Churches Dependent on the Congregation for the Evangelisation of Peoples*, 3.

Therefore, no one may licitly change what Christ has willed for his Church. It is indissolubly bound with its Founder and Head, who alone may provide her, through the power of the Holy Spirit, with ministers in the service of the faithful. Taking the place of Christ who calls, consecrates and sends forth through legitimate Pastors may be no community, which, albeit in situations of particular necessity, might wish to give itself its own priest in ways contrary to the dispositions of the Church: the priesthood is a choice of Jesus, not of the community (cf. *Jn* 15:16). The response to cases of necessity is the prayer of Jesus: "Pray, therefore, the Lord of the harvest, that he send forth labourers to his harvest!" (*Mt* 9:38). If added to this prayer made with faith is the community's intense life of charity, we can be sure that the Lord will not fail to give pastors according to his heart (cf. *Jer* 3:15)[116].

28. In order to safeguard the order established by the Lord Jesus it is also necessary to avoid the so-called "clericalisation" of the laity[117], which tends to compress the ministerial priesthood of the priest, attributed to whom alone, after the Bishop and by virtue of the priestly ministry received with ordination, may be the term "pastor" in a proper and univocal sense. The attribute "pastoral", in fact, refers to participation in the Episcopal ministry.

## 1.5. Priestly Communion

*Communion with the Trinity and with Christ*

29. In light of what has been said above about identity, the communion of the priest is fulfilled above all with the Father, the ultimate origin of all his power; with the Son, in whose redemptive mission he participates; with the Holy Spirit, who gives him the power for living and fulfilling that pastoral char-

---

[116] Cf. ECUMENICAL COUNCIL VATICAN II, Decree *Presbyterorum Ordinis*, 11.

[117] Cf. JOHN PAUL II, *Address to the Episcopacy of Switzerland* (15 June 1984): *Insegnamenti* VII/1 (1984), 1784.

ity, which, as "the internal principle, the force which animates and guides the spiritual life of the priest"[118], qualifies him in a priestly way. A pastoral charity which, far from being reduced to a series of techniques and methods serving the functional efficacy of the ministry, refers to the nature proper of the mission of the Church for the salvation of humanity.

Indeed, "the nature and mission of the ministerial priesthood cannot be defined except through this multiple and rich interconnection of relationships which arise from the Blessed Trinity and are prolonged in the communion of the Church, as a sign and instrument of Christ, of communion with God and of the unity of all humanity"[119].

## Communion with the Church

30. Issuing forth for the priest from this fundamental union-communion with Christ and the Trinity is his communion-relation with the Church in its aspects of mystery and ecclesial community[120].

Concretely, the ecclesial communion of the priest is lived in diverse ways. In fact, through sacramental ordination he develops special bonds with the *Pope, the Episcopal Body, his own Bishop, other priests and the lay faithful.*

## Hierarchical Communion

31. Communion as a characteristic of the priesthood is based on the oneness of the Head, Pastor and Spouse of the Church, who is Christ[121].

---

[118]    JOHN PAUL II, Post-Synodal Apostolic Exhortation *Pastores dabo vobis,* 23.

[119]    JOHN PAUL II, Post-Synodal Apostolic Exhortation *Pastores dabo vobis,* 12; cf. ECUMENICAL COUNCIL VATICAN II, Dogmatic Constitution *Lumen gentium,* 1.

[120]    Cf. ECUMENICAL COUNCIL VATICAN II, Dogmatic Constitution *Lumen gentium,* 8.

[121]    Cf. ST. AUGUSTINE, *Sermo* 46, 30: *CCL* 41, 555-557.

Taking form in said ministerial communion are also some precise ties first of all with the Pope, the College of Bishops and his own Bishop. "There can be no genuine priestly ministry except in communion with the supreme pontiff and the episcopal college, especially with one's own diocesan bishop, who deserves that 'filial respect and obedience' promised during the rite of ordination"[122]. This is therefore a hierarchical communion, that is to say, a communion in that hierarchy in the same way in which it is structured internally.

In virtue of participation in a degree subordinate to the Bishops – who are invested with power "proper, ordinary, and immediate, although its exercise is ultimately controlled by the supreme authority of the Church"[123] – in the one ministerial priesthood, the said communion also involves the spiritual and organic-structural bond of priests with the entire Episcopal order and with the Roman Pontiff. This is reinforced by the fact that the entire Episcopal order as a whole, and each Bishop individually, must be in hierarchical communion with the Head of the College[124]. In fact, this College is composed only of those consecrated Bishops who are in hierarchical communion with its Head and members.

## Communion in the Eucharistic Celebration

32. Hierarchical communion is most meaningfully expressed in the Eucharistic prayers, when the priest, praying for the Pope, the College of Bishops and his own Bishop, expresses not only a sentiment of devotion, but attests to the authenticity of his celebration as well[125].

---

[122] JOHN PAUL II, Post-Synodal Apostolic Exhortation *Pastores dabo vobis*, 28.

[123] ECUMENICAL COUNCIL VATICAN II, Dogmatic Constitution *Lumen gentium*, 27.

[124] Cf. ECUMENICAL COUNCIL VATICAN II, Dogmatic Constitution *Lumen gentium*, 22; Decree *Christus Dominus*, 4; *C.I.C.*, can. 336.

[125] Cf. CONGREGATION FOR THE DOCTRINE OF THE FAITH, Letter on the Church as Communion, *Communionis notio*, 14.

The Eucharistic concelebration itself, in the circumstances and conditions foreseen[126], when presided over by the Bishop and with the participation of the faithful, manifests the unity of the priesthood of Christ in the plurality of his ministers, as well as the unity of the sacrifice of the People of God[127]. Moreover, it contributes to the consolidation of the ministerial fraternity existing among priests[128].

*Communion in the Exercise of the Ministry*

33. Each priest is to have a deep, humble and filial bond of obedience and charity with the person of the Holy Father and adhere to his Petrine ministry of *Magisterium*, sanctification and government with exemplary docility[129].

Filial union with his own Bishop is also an indispensable condition for the efficacy of the priestly ministry. For pastors with more experience it is easy to note the need to avoid any form of subjectivism in the exercise of the sacred ministry and adhere in a co-responsible manner to pastoral programmes. Besides being an expression of maturity, this adhesion, which entails proceeding in unison with the mind of the Bishop, con-tributes to the edification of that unity in communion which is indispensable for the work of evangelisation[130].

With full respect for hierarchical subordination, the priest will promote a genuine relationship with his Bishop character-

---

[126]    Cf. *C.I.C.,* can. 902; SACRED CONGREGATION FOR THE SACRA-MENTS AND DIVINE WORSHIP, Decree *Promulgato Codice* (12 September 1983), II, I, 153: *Notitiae* 19 (1983), 542.

[127]    Cf. ST. THOMAS AQUINAS, *Summa theol.,* III, q. 82, a. 2 ad 2; *Sent.* IV, d. 13, q. 1, a 2, q. 2; ECUMENICAL COUNCIL VATICAN II, Constitution *Sacrosanctum Concilium,* 41, 57.

[128]    Cf. SACRED CONGREGATION FOR RITES, Instruction *Eucharisticum Mysterium* (25 May 1967), 47: *AAS* 59 (1967), 565-566.

[129]    Cf. *C.I.C.* can. 273.

[130]    Cf. ECUMENICAL COUNCIL VATICAN II, Decree *Presbyterorum Ordinis,* 15; JOHN PAUL II, Post-Synodal Apostolic Exhortation *Pastores dabo vobis,* 65; 79.

ised by sincere trustfulness, cordial friendship, prayer for his person and intentions, and a true effort of consonance and convergence in ideals and programmes, which takes nothing away from intelligent capacity for personal initiative and pastoral resourcefulness[131].

In view of his own spiritual and pastoral growth, and out of love for his flock, the priest should welcome with gratitude, and even seek on a regular basis, the orientations of his bishop or the latter's representatives for the development of his pastoral ministry. It is also an admirable practice for the priest to request the opinions of more expert priests and qualified laypersons with respect to the most suitable pastoral methods.

*Communion in the Presbyterate*

34. By virtue of the Sacrament of Holy Orders "each priest is united to the other members of the priesthood by specific bonds of apostolic charity, ministry and fraternity"[132]. In fact, he is inserted into the *Ordo Presbyterorum* constituting that unity which can be defined as a true family in which the ties are not of flesh or blood, but come from the grace of Holy Orders[133]. Belonging to a specific presbyterate[134] always takes

---

[131]    ST. IGNATIUS OF ANTIOCH, *Ad Ephesios*, XX, 1-2: "[...] If the Lord will reveal to me that, each one on his own and everyone together [...] you are united in the heart through an unshakeable submission to the Bishop and the presbyterate, breaking the only bread which is remedy of immortality, an antidote to prevent death, and to live forever in Jesus Christ": *Patres Apostolici*, ed. F.X. FUNK, II, 203-205.

[132]    JOHN PAUL II, Post-Synodal Apostolic Exhortation *Pastores dabo vobis*, 17; cf. ECUMENICAL COUNCIL VATICAN II, Dogmatic Constitution *Lumen gentium*, 28; Decree *Presbyterorum Ordinis*, 8; *C.I.C.*, can. 275, § 1.

[133]    Cf. JOHN PAUL II, Post-Synodal Apostolic Exhortation *Pastores dabo vobis*, 74; CONGREGATION FOR THE EVANGELISATION OF THE PEOPLES, *Pastoral Guide for Diocesan Priests of the Churches Dependent on the Congregation for the Evangelisation of Peoples* (1 October, 1989), 6.

[134]    Cf. ECUMENICAL COUNCIL VATICAN II, Decree *Presbyterorum Ordinis*, 8; *C.I.C.*, canons 369; 498; 499.

place within the context of a particular Church, an Ordinariate or a personal Prelature – that is to say in the context of an "Episcopal mission", and not for reasons of incardination – which in no way alters the fact that the priest, he too a baptised person, belongs in an immediate manner to the universal Church: no one is a stranger in the Church; the entire Church, and each diocese, is family, the family of God[135].

Priestly fraternity and membership in a presbyterate are therefore elements characterising the priest. The rite of the imposition of the hands during the priestly ordination by the Bishop and all the priests present harbours special significance insofar as it indicates both equality of participation in the ministry and the fact that the priest cannot act by himself, but always within the presbyterate, becoming a brother of all those who constitute it[136].

"Bishops and priests receive the mission and the faculty [the 'sacred power'] to act *'in Persona Christi Capitis'*, deacons the force to serve the People of God in the *'diaconia'* of the liturgy, the word and charity in communion with the Bishop and his presbyterate"[137].

*Incardination, an Authentic Juridical Bond with Spiritual Value*

35. Incardination in a determined "particular Church or in a personal Prelature or in an institute of consecrated life or in a society which has this faculty"[138] constitutes a genuine juridical

---

[135]   Cf. ECUMENICAL COUNCIL VATICAN II, Dogmatic Constitution *Lumen gentium*, 6; BENEDICT XVI, *Angelus* (19 June 2005): *Insegnamenti* I (2005), 255-256; JOHN PAUL II, Post-Synodal Apostolic Exhortation *Ecclesia in Africa* (14 September 1995): *AAS* 88 (1996), 63.

[136]   Cf. *Pontificale Romanum, De Ordinatione Episcopi, Presbyterorum et Diaconorum*, cap. II, 105; 130; ECUMENICAL COUNCIL VATICAN II, Decree *Presbyterorum Ordinis*, 8.

[137]   *Catechism of the Catholic Church*, 875.

[138]   *C.I.C.*, can. 265.

bond[139], which also has a spiritual value insofar as issuing forth there from is "the priest's relationship with his bishop in the one presbyterate, his sharing in the bishop's ecclesial concern and his devotion to the evangelical care of the People of God in specific historical and contextual conditions. . ."[140].

In this regard it should not be forgotten that the secular priests not incardinated in the Diocese and the priest members of a religious institute or a society of apostolic life who live in the Diocese and for its good exercise some office in it, although still subject to their respective legitimate Ordinary, belong by full or diverse title to the clergy of said Diocese[141], where "they have the right to both an active and a passive voice in an election to the council of priests"[142]. The religious priests, in particular, by virtue of unity of forces share pastoral solicitude, offering the contribution of specific charisms and "with their presence inspiring the particular Church to live more vividly its universal openness"[143].

The priests incardinated in a Diocese, but serving an ecclesial movement or new community approved by the competent ecclesial Authority[144], are to be aware of being members of the presbyterate of the diocese where they conduct their ministry, and are duty bound to collaborate with it. In his turn, the Bishop of incardination is to foster the legally recognised right of the faithful to their form of spiritual life[145], which the law recognises as the right of all the faithful, respect the way of life required by membership in a Movement, and be prepared,

---

[139]   Cf. JOHN PAUL II, *Address in the Cathedral of Quito to Bishops, Priests, Religious and Seminarians* (29 January 1985): *Insegnamenti* VIII/1 (1985), 247-253. JOHN PAUL II, Post-Synodal Apostolic Exhortation *Pastores dabo vobis*, 31.

[141]   Cf. *ibid.*, 17; 74.

[142]   *C.I.C.*, can. 498, § 1, 2°.

[143]   JOHN PAUL II, Post-Synodal Apostolic Exhortation *Pastores dabo vobis* , 31.

[144]   Cf. *ibid.,* 31; 41; 68.

[145]   Cf. *C.I.C.*, cann. 214-215.

pursuant to law in force, to permit the priest to exercise his service in other local Churches if this forms part of the charism of the movement itself[146], while ever striving to strengthen ecclesial communion.

*The Presbyterate: a Place of Sanctification*

36. The presbyterate is the privileged place where the priest should be able to find specific means of formation, sanctification and evangelisation, and be helped to overcome the limits and weaknesses proper to human nature.

He will therefore make every effort to avoid living his priestly service in an isolated and subjectivist manner, and will seek to promote fraternal communion by giving and receiving – from priest to priest – the warmth of friendship, caring assistance, acceptance and fraternal correction[147], well aware that the grace of the Order "takes up and elevates the human and psychological bonds of affection and friendship, as well as the spiritual bonds which exist between priests [...] and find expression in the most varied forms of mutual assistance, spiritual and material as well"[148].

In addition to its expression in the Chrism Mass – the manifestation of the communion of priests with their Bishop – all this is expressed in the liturgy of the Mass *In Coena Domini* of Holy Thursday, which shows how through Eucharistic communion – born in the Last Supper – priests receive the capacity to love one another, as the Master loves them[149].

[146] Cf. *C.I.C.*, can. 271.

[147] Cf. BENEDICT XVI, *Message for Lent 2012* (3 November 2011): *AAS* 104 (2012), 199-204.

[148] JOHN PAUL II, Post-Synodal Apostolic Exhortation *Pastores dabo vobis*, 74.

[149] JOHN PAUL II, *General Audience* (4 August 1993), 4: *Insegnamenti* XVI/2, 139-140.

*Fraternal Priestly Friendship*

37. The profound and ecclesial sense of the presbyterate not only fails to hamper, but actually fosters the personal responsibility of each priest in carrying out the particular ministry entrusted to him by the Bishop[150]. The capacity to cultivate and live deep priestly friendships proves to be a source of serenity and joy in the exercise of the ministry, a decisive form of support in difficulties, and valuable help for growth in the pastoral charity which the priest must exercise in a particular way towards those confreres in difficulty and in need of understanding, assistance and support[151]. Priestly fraternity is an expression of the law of charity and, far from being little more than a mere sentiment, becomes for priests an existential remembrance of Christ and apostolic witness of ecclesial communion.

*Common Life*

38. A manifestation of this communion is also the *common life* always supported by the Church[152], recently emphasized by the documents of the Second Vatican Ecumenical Council[153] and the successive *Magisterium*[154], and applied in many dioceses with positive results. "The common life expresses a form of help Christ gives to our existence, calling us, through the presence of brothers, to a increasingly deeper configuration of his

---

[150]    Cf. ECUMENICAL COUNCIL VATICAN II, Decree *Presbyterorum Ordinis*, 12-14.

[151]    Cf. *ibid.*, 8.

[152]    Cf. ST. AUGUSTINE, *Sermones* 355, 356, *De vita et moribus clericorum*: PL 39, 1568-1581.

[153]    Cf. ECUMENICAL COUNCIL VATICAN II, Dogmatic Constitution *Lumen gentium* 28; Decree *Presbyterorum Ordinis* 8; Decree *Christus Dominus* 30.

[154]    Cf. SACRED CONGREGATION OF BISHOPS, Directory *Ecclesiae Imago* (22 February 1973), 112; CONGREGATION FOR BISHOPS, Directory *Apostolorum Successores* for the Pastoral Ministry of Bishops (22 February 2004), LEV, Vatican City 2004, 211; *C.I.C.*, cann. 280; 245, § 2; 550, § 1; JOHN PAUL II, Post-Synodal Apostolic Exhortation *Pastores dabo vobis*, 81.

person. Living with others means accepting the need for one's ongoing conversion, and especially discovering the beauty of such a journey, the joy of humility, repentance, but also conversion, mutual forgiveness and reciprocal support. *Ecce quae bonum et quam iucundum habitare fratres in unum (Ps* 133:1)"[155].

In order to tackle one of the most important problems facing priestly life today, that being the solitude of the priest, "one cannot sufficiently recommend to priests a life lived in common and directed entirely towards their sacred ministry, the practice of having frequent meetings with a fraternal exchange of ideas, counsel and experience with their brother priests, the movement to form associations which encourage priestly holiness"[156].

39. Among the diverse forms of common life (residence, community at table, etc.), held in eminent pride of place is to be communal participation in liturgical prayer[157]. Its diverse modalities are to be encouraged according to possibilities and practical conditions, without necessarily transferring the albeit praiseworthy models proper to the religious life. Worthy of praise in particular are those associations which support priestly fraternity, holiness in the exercise of the ministry, and communion with the Bishop and the entire Church[158].

Considering how important it is for priests to live in the vicinity of where those whom they serve abide, it is hoped that the pastors of parishes will be willing to foster common life in the parochial house with their vicars[159], effectively considering them as their co-workers and sharers of pastoral solicitude; in

---

[155]   BENEDICT XVI, *Private Audience with the Priests of the Fraternity of St. Charles on the Occasion of the XXV of Foundation* (12 February 2011): "L'Osservatore Romano", 13 February 2011, 8.

[156]   PAUL VI, Encyclical Letter *Sacerdotalis caelibatus*, 80.

[157]   Cf. ECUMENICAL COUNCIL VATICAN II, Constitution *Sacrosanctum Concilium* 26; 99; *Institutio Generalis Liturgiae Horarum*, 25.

[158]   Cf. *C.I.C.*, can. 278, § 2; JOHN PAUL II, Post-Synodal Apostolic Exhortation *Pastores dabo vobis*, 31; 68; 81.

[159]   Cf. *C.I.C.*, can. 550, § 2.

their turn, the vicars, in order to build up priestly communion, must recognise and respect the authority of the parish priest[160]. In cases where there is only one priest in a parish, the possibility of a common life with other priests in neighbouring parishes is highly encouraged[161].

The experience of this common life has been rather positive in many places because it has represented a real form of support for priests: created is a family environment, with the permission of the local Ordinary[162] it is possible to have a chapel for the Blessed Sacrament, and it is also possible to pray together, etc. Moreover, as we learn from the experience and teachings of the saints, "no one can assume the regenerating force of the common life without prayer [...], without a sacramental life lived with fidelity. Unless one enters into the eternal dialogue the Son has with the Father in the Holy Spirit, no authentic common life is possible. It is necessary to be with Jesus in order to be able to be with others"[163]. Many are the cases of priests who have found an important source of help for both their personal needs and the exercise of their pastoral ministry in the adoption of opportune forms of communitarian life.

40. The common life is an image of that *apostolica vivendi forma* of Jesus with his apostles. With the gift of sacred celibacy for the Kingdom of Heaven, the Lord has made us become members of his family in a special way. In a society so strongly marked by individualism, the priest needs a deeper personal relationship and a vital space characterised by fraternal friendship where he may live as a Christian and a priest: "moments of

---

[160]   Cf. *ibid.*, can. 545, § 1.

[161]   Cf. *ibid.*, can. 533, § 1.

[162]   Cf. *ibid.*, cann. 1226; 1228.

[163]   BENEDICT XVI, *Private Audience with the Priests of the Fraternity of St. Charles on the Occasion of the XXV of Foundation* (12 February 2011): "L'Osservatore Romano", 13 February 2011, 8.

prayer and study in common, the sharing of the demands of life and priestly work are a necessary part of your life"[164].

In this atmosphere of mutual assistance the priest thereby finds terrain suited to persevering in the vocation of service to the Church: "In the company of Christ and his brother priests, each priest can find the energies needed to take care of his fellow men, take upon himself the spiritual and material needs he encounters, and with ever new words dictated by love teach the eternal truths of the faith to those who thirst, also among our contemporaries"[165].

In the priestly prayer at the Last Supper Jesus prayed for the unity of his disciples: "May they all be one. Father, may they be one in us, as you are in me and I am in you" (*Jn* 17:21). Each expression of communion in the Church "stems from the unity of the Father, the Son and the Holy Spirit"[166]. Priests are to be convinced that their fraternal communion, especially in common life, constitutes witness in keeping with what Jesus made so clear in his prayer to the Father: may the disciples be one so the world "may believe that you sent me" (*Jn* 17:21) and know that "I have loved them as much as you loved me" (*Jn* 17:23). "Jesus calls on the priestly community to be the reflection of and participation in Trinitarian communion: what a sublime ideal!"[167].

*Communion with the Lay Faithful*

41. As a man of communion, the priest will not be able to express his love for the Lord and for the Church without

---

[164] BENEDICT XVI, *Homily on the Occasion of the Celebration of Vespers* (Fatima, 12 May 2010): *Insegnamenti* VI/1 (2010), 685-688.

[165] BENEDICT XVI, *Private Audience with the Priests of the Fraternity of St. Charles on the Occasion of the XXV of Foundation* (12 February 2011): *l.c.*, 8.

[166] ST. CYPRIAN, *De Oratione Domini*, 23: PL 4, 553; ECUMENICAL COUNCIL VATICAN II, Dogmatic Constitution *Lumen gentium*, 4.

[167] JOHN PAUL II, *General Audience* (4 August 1993), 4: *Insegnamenti* XVI/2, 139-140.

translating it into factual and unconditional love for all Christians, the object of his pastoral care[168].

Like Christ, he must make Christ "visible in the midst of the flock" entrusted to his care[169], creating a positive relationship between himself and the lay faithful; recognising their dignity as children of God, he fosters their role in the Church and places at their service everything of his priestly ministry and pastoral charity[170]. This attitude of love and charity is far removed from the so-called "laicisation of priests", which actually waters down in priests what constitutes their identity: the faithful ask priests to show themselves for who they are, both externally and interiorly, at all times, in all places and under all circumstances. A precious occasion for the evangelising mission of the shepherd of souls is the traditional annual visit and Easter blessing of families.

A distinctive manifestation of this dimension in building up the Christian community consists in transcending any particularist attitude: in fact, priests must never place themselves at the service of a particular ideology insofar as this would wane the efficacy of their ministry. The priest's relationship with the faithful must always be essentially priestly.

In the awareness of the profound communion that binds him to the lay faithful and to religious, the priest will deploy every effort "to awaken and deepen co-responsibility in the one and common and single mission of salvation, with prompt and heartfelt esteem for all the charisms and tasks which the Spirit gives believers for the building up of the Church"[171].

---

[168] Cf. JOHN PAUL II, *General Audience* (7 July 1993): *Insegnamenti* XVI/2, 34-44; ECUMENICAL COUNCIL VATICAN II, Decree *Presbyterorum Ordinis*, 15.

[169] JOHN PAUL II, Post-Synodal Apostolic Exhortation *Pastores dabo vobis*, 15.

[170] Cf. ECUMENICAL COUNCIL VATICAN II, Decree *Presbyterorum Ordinis*, 9; *C.I.C.*, cann. 275, § 2; 529, § 2.

[171] JOHN PAUL II, Post-Synodal Apostolic Exhortation *Pastores dabo vobis*, 74.

More specifically, the parish priest, in his constant quest for the common good of the Church, will encourage associations of the faithful and the movements or the new communities that have religious purposes[172], embracing them all and helping them to find unity of intentions among themselves in prayer and apostolic enterprise.

One of the tasks that demands special attention is the formation of the laity. The priest cannot be satisfied with the laity having a superficial knowledge of the faith, but must seek to give them a solid formation, persevering in his efforts through theology lessons and courses on Christian doctrine, especially through study of the *Catechism of the Catholic Church* and its *Compendium*. Such formation will help the laity to expedite in full their role as Christian animators of the temporal order (political, cultural, economic, social)[173]. Moreover, entrusted in certain cases to laypersons with sufficient formation and a sincere desire to serve the Church may be some tasks – in accord with the laws of the Church – that do not pertain exclusively to the priestly ministry, and which they can perform on the basis of their professional and personal experience. In this manner the priest will be freer in attending to his primary commitments such as preaching, the celebration of the Sacraments and spiritual direction. In this sense one of the important tasks for parish priests is to discover among the faithful persons with the skills, virtues and a coherent Christian life – for example, as regards matrimony – who can provide an efficient and helping hand in pastoral activities: the preparation of children for First Communion and first Confession or youngsters for Confirmation, the family apostolate, pre-marriage catechesis, etc. There can be no doubt that concern for the formation of these persons – who are models for many other persons – and the fact of helping them in their journey of faith will have to be one of the main apprehensions of priests.

---

[172]   Cf. *C.I.C.*, can. 529, § 2.
[173]   Cf. ECUMENICAL COUNCIL VATICAN II, Dogmatic Constitution *Lumen gentium*, 31.

Insofar as he unites the family of God and brings Church-communion into being, the priest – well aware of the great gift of his vocation – becomes the "pontifex", he who unites man to God, becoming the brother of his fellowmen in the selfsame act with which he wishes to be their pastor, father and master[174]. For the man of today who seeks the sense of his existence, he is the Good Shepherd and guide leading to the encounter with Christ, an encounter that takes place as announcement and as reality already present in the Church, albeit not in a definitive manner. In this manner the priest, placed at the service of the People of God, will present himself as an expert in humanity, a man of truth and communion, a witness of the solicitude of the Only Shepherd for each and every member of his flock. The community will be able to count on his availability, his work of evangelisation, and above all his faithful and unconditional love. The manifestation of this love will mainly be his dedication in preaching, in the celebration of the Sacraments, especially the Eucharist and Penance, and in spiritual direction as a means for helping to discern the signs of God's will[175]. Revealing himself at all times as priest, he will therefore exercise his spiritual mission with kindness and firmness, humility and a spirit of service[176], opening himself to compassion, participating in the sufferings inflicted upon men by the various forms of poverty, spiritual and material, old and new. He will also know how to bend over with mercy upon the difficult and uncertain journey of the conversion of sinners, to whom he will reserve the gift of truth and the patient, encouraging benevolence of the Good Shepherd, who does not re-

---

[174] Cf. JOHN PAUL II, Post-Synodal Apostolic Exhortation *Pastores dabo vobis*, 74; PAUL VI, Encyclical Letter *Ecclesiam suam* (6 August 1964), III: *AAS* 56 (1964), 647.

[175] Cf. CONGREGATION FOR THE CLERGY, *The Priest, Minister of Divine Mercy. Material for Confessors and Spiritual Directors* (9 March 2011): booklet, LEV, Vatican City 2011.

[176] Cf. JOHN PAUL II, *General Audience* (7 July 1993): *l.c.*, 34-44.

prove the lost sheep, but loads it onto his shoulders and celebrates its return to the fold (cf. *Lk* 15:4-7)[177].

It is a matter of affirming the charity of Christ as the origin and perfect realisation of the new man (cf. *Eph* 2:15), of what man is in his full truth. In the life of a priest this charity becomes an authentic passion that explicitly configures his ministry for the generation of the Christian people.

### Communion with the Members of Institutes of Consecrated Life

42. The priest will dedicate particular attention to relations with brothers and sisters engaged in the life of special consecration to God in all its forms, showing them sincere appreciation and a real spirit of apostolic collaboration, respecting and prompting their specific charisms. Moreover, he will cooperate so the consecrated life may appear ever more luminous for the good of the entire Church, and increasingly persuasive and attractive for the new generations.

In this spirit of esteem for the consecrated life the priest will extend special care to those communities which for diverse reasons are in greater need of good doctrine, assistance and encouragement in both fidelity and the promotion of vocations.

### Vocational Activity

43. Each priest will devote special dedication to vocational activity, never failing to encourage prayers for vocations, sparing no pains in catechesis, attending to the formation of altar servers and fostering suitable endeavours through a personal relationship helping to discover talents and being able to discover God's will for a courageous choice in the following of Christ[178]. Fundamentally important in this work are families, which constitute the domestic churches where young people

---

[177]   Cf. *C.I.C.*, can. 529, § 1.
[178]   Cf. ECUMENICAL COUNCIL VATICAN II, Decree *Presbyterorum Ordinis*, 11; *C.I.C.*, can. 233, § 1.

learn how to pray, grow in virtue and be generous from a very early age. Priests are to encourage Christian spouses to configure the home as a true school of Christian life, pray together with their children, ask God to call someone to follow him by his side with an undivided heart (*1Cor* 7:32-34), and be ever joyful over vocations that may arise from within their own family.

This activity will have to be founded primarily on the greatness of the call, his divine election for the good of man: to be brought first and foremost to the attention of young people is how precious and beautiful is the gift of following Christ. This is why most important is the role incumbent upon the ordained minister through the example of his faith and his life: the priest's clear knowledge of his identity, the coherence of his life, and his transparent joy and missionary ardour constitute absolutely necessary elements of that vocation promotion activity, which must be an integral part of the organic and ordinary pastoral ministry. Therefore, the joyful manifestation of his adhesion to the mystery of Jesus, his prayerful attitude, and the care and devotion with which he celebrates Holy Mass and the sacraments irradiate that example which fascinates young people.

Moreover, the lengthy experience of the life of the Church underscores how necessary it is to attend to the formation of young people from an early age, doing so with patience and tenacity, and never yielding to discouragement. In this way they will have those spiritual resources needed to respond to an eventual call from God. For this it is indispensable – and this should be part of any vocation promotion activity – to foment within them the life of prayer and intimacy with God, recourse to the sacraments, especially the Eucharist and confession, and spiritual direction as help for making progress in the interior life. In a suitable and generous manner priests will thereby kindle the vocational proposal in young people who may seem well disposed. Even though it must be constant, this engagement will become more intense especially under certain circumstances, such as, for example, retreats, preparation for confirmation, or when working with altar servers.

The priest will always maintain relations of cordial collaboration and sincere affection with the seminary, the cradle of his own vocation and the training grounds for his first experience of communal life.

It is "a necessary requirement of pastoral charity"[179], of love for one's priesthood for each priest – ever docile to the grace of the Holy Spirit – to be concerned about inspiring vocations to the priesthood that may continue his ministry at the service of the Lord and for the good of humanity.

## Political and Social Engagement

44. The priest is a servant of the Church, which by virtue of its universality and catholicity cannot have ties with any historical contingency, and hence he will therefore remain above and beyond any political party. He may not play an active role in political parties or the management of labour unions, unless, according to the judgement of the competent ecclesiastical authority, the rights of the Church and the promotion of the common good so require[180]. In fact, even though these are good things in their own right, they are nonetheless alien to the clerical state since they can constitute a grave danger of division of ecclesial communion[181].

Just like Jesus (cf. *Jn* 6:15 ff), the priest "must forego engagement in forms of active politics, especially when biased as almost inevitably occurs, in order to remain the man of all from the viewpoint of spiritual fraternity"[182]. Therefore, all the

---

[179]    JOHN PAUL II, Post-Synodal Apostolic Exhortation *Pastores dabo vobis*, 74.

[180]    Cf. *C.I.C.*, can. 287, § 2; SACRED CONGREGATION FOR THE CLERGY, Decree *Quidam Episcopi* (8 March 1982), *AAS* 74 (1982), 642-645.

[181]    Cf. CONGREGATION FOR THE EVANGELISATION OF PEOPLES, *Pastoral Guide for the Diocesan Priests of the Churches Dependent on the Congregation for the Evangelisation of Peoples*, 9: *l.c.*, 1604-1607; SACRED CONGREGATION FOR THE CLERGY, Decree *Quidam Episcopi* (8 March 1982), *l.c.*, 642-645.

[182]    JOHN PAUL II, *General Audience* (28 July 1993), 3: *Insegnamenti* XVI/2, 109-110; cf. ECUMENICAL COUNCIL VATICAN II, Pastoral

faithful must always be able to approach the priest without feeling inhibited for any reason.

The priest will remember that "it is not the role of the Pastors of the Church to intervene directly in the political structuring and organisation of social life. This task is part of the vocation of the lay faithful, acting on their own initiative with their fellow citizens"[183]; nonetheless, following the criteria of the *Magisterium*, he will not fail to attend to the correct formation of their conscience"[184]. The priest therefore bears special responsibility for explaining, promoting, and, if necessary, defending – always pursuant to the orientations of the law and the *Magisterium* of the Church – religious and moral truths, also in the presence of public opinion, and even in the vast world of the mass media if he does have the specific preparation necessary. In an increasingly secularised culture where religion is often disregarded and considered as irrelevant or illegitimate in social debate, or at the most relegated to the intimacy of consciences alone, the priest is called to sustain the public and community significance of the Christian faith, transmitting it in a clear and convincing manner on all occasions, welcome or unwelcome (cf. *2Tm* 4:2), and keeping ever in mind that patrimony of teachings that constitutes the Social Doctrine of the Church. The *Compendium of the Social Doctrine of the Church* is an incisive instrument that will help him to present this social teaching and illustrate its richness in today's social context.

The reduction of his mission to temporal tasks of a purely social or political nature, or in any case alien to his identity, would be not a conquest but a most grave loss for the evangelical fecundity of the entire Church.

---

Constitution *Gaudium et spes*, 43; SYNOD OF BISHOPS, Document on the Ministerial Priesthood *Ultimis temporibus* (30 November 1971), II, I, 2: *l.c.*, 912-913; *C.I.C.*, cann. 285, § 3; 287, § 1.

[183] *Catechism of the Catholic Church*, 2442; *C.I.C.*, can. 227.

[184] SYNOD OF BISHOPS, Document on the Ministerial Priesthood *Ultimis temporibus* (30 November 1971), II, I, 2: *l.c.*, 913.

# II. PRIESTLY SPIRITUALITY

The spirituality of the priest consists essentially in the profound relationship of friendship with Christ, because he is called "to go to Him" (cf. *Mk* 3:13). In this sense, in the life of the priest, Jesus will always have pre-eminence over everything. Each priest acts within a particular historical context with its manifold challenges and requirements. Precisely for this reason is the guarantee of the fecundity of his ministry rooted in a deep interior life. If the priest does not count on the primacy of grace he will not be able to respond to the challenges of his times, and any pastoral programme is destined to failure, no matter how elaborate it may be.

## 2.1. The Current Historical Context

*Being Able to Interpret the Signs of the Times*

45. The life and ministry of priests unfold within a particular historical context, at times replete with new problems and unprecedented resources, and in which the pilgrim Church lives in the world.

The priesthood is born not of history, but of the immutable will of God. Nonetheless, it interacts with historical circumstances and – while remaining ever identical – assumes tangible form in the concreteness of choices also through an evangelical reading of "the signs of the times". For this reason it is the duty of priests to interpret such "signs" in the light of the faith and submit them to prudent discernment. In any case, priests will not be able to ignore them, especially if they wish to orient their life in an efficacious and germane way in order to render their service and their witness for the Kingdom of God fruitful.

In the current phase of the life of the Church, with the social context marked by intense secularism and after proposed anew to all has been a "lofty measure" of the ordinary Christian life in the sense of holiness[185], priests are called to live their ministry in depth as witnesses of hope and transcendence, ever taking into consideration the increasingly numerous and delicate demands they must face, not only of a pastoral nature, but likewise social and cultural[186].

They are therefore engaged today in diverse fields of the apostolate that require total generosity and dedication, intellectual preparation, and above all a mature and deep spiritual life rooted in pastoral charity, which is their specific way to holiness and also constitutes an authentic service to the faithful in the pastoral ministry. In this manner, and despite their limitations, if they strive to live their consecration in full – remaining united to Christ and letting themselves be permeated by his Spirit – they will be able to carry out their ministry, helped by the grace in which they will place their trust. To this grace must they have recourse, "aware of being able to tend to perfection with the hope of progressing more and more in holiness"[187].

## The Demand of Conversion for Evangelisation

46. It is therefore clear that the priest is involved in a very special way in the commitment of the entire Church for evangelisation. Beginning from faith in Jesus Christ, the Redeemer of mankind, the priest is assured that in Him there are "unfathomable treasures" (*Eph* 3:8), which no culture or era can ex-

---

[185]    Cf. JOHN PAUL II, Apostolic Letter *Novo millennio ineunte*, *l.c.*; BENEDICT XVI, *General Audience* (13 April 2011): "L'Osservatore Romano", 14 April 2011, 8.

[186]    Cf. JOHN PAUL II, Post-Synodal Apostolic Exhortation *Pastores dabo vobis*, 5.

[187]    JOHN PAUL II, *General Audience* (26 May 1993): *Insegnamenti* XVI/1 (1993), 1328-1340.

haust, and which men can always draw upon for their enrichment[188].

This is therefore the time for a renewal of our faith in Jesus Christ, who is the same "yesterday, today and for ever!" (*Heb* 13:8). Hence, "the call to the new evangelisation is first of all a call to conversion"[189]. At one and the same time it is a call to that hope "which rests upon the promises of God, on fidelity to his Word, and which as an unshakeable uncertainty has the resurrection of Christ, his definitive victory over sin and death, the first announcement and root of all evangelisation, the foundation of all human promotion, and the starting point of every authentic Christian culture"[190].

In this context the priest must above all revive his faith, his hope, and his sincere love for the Lord, in such way as to be able to present Him to the contemplation of the faithful and all men as He truly is: a Person alive and fascinating, who loves us more than anyone else because He gave His life for us: "A man can have no greater love than to lay down his life for his friends" (*Jn* 15:13).

At the same time the priest should act under the impetus of a receptive and joyful spirit, the fruit of his union with God through prayer and sacrifice, which is an essential element of his evangelising mission of becoming all for everyone (cf. *1 Cor* 9:19-23) in order to win them over to Christ. In the same way, aware of the undeserved mercy of God in his life and in the life of his brothers, he must cultivate the virtues of humility and compassion towards the People of God at large, especially those who feel themselves extraneous to the Church. Conscious of the fact that each person is looking in diverse ways for a love able to bring him beyond the august confines of human weakness, egoism and above all death itself, the priest

---

[188]  Cf. JOHN PAUL II, *Inaugural Address to the IV General Conference of the Latin American Episcopate* (Santo Domingo, 12-28 October 1992), 24: *AAS* 85 (1993), 826.

[189]  *Ibid.*, 1.

[190]  *Ibid.*, 25.

will proclaim that Jesus Christ is the response to all these yearnings.

In the new evangelisation the priest is called to be *the herald of hope*[191], which issues forth also from the awareness that he himself was touched by the Lord first: in himself he lives the joy of the salvation offered to him by Jesus. This is a hope not only of the mind, but also of the heart, because the priest has been touched by the love of Christ: "You did not choose me, no, I chose you" (*Jn* 15:16).

## The Challenge of Sects and New Cults

47. The proliferation of sects and new cults, as well as their diffusion among the Catholic faithful, constitutes a special challenge for the pastoral ministry. At the root of these phenomena lie complex causes. In any case, the priestly ministry is summoned to respond promptly and incisively to the search for sacredness, and in particular to the search for authentic spirituality emerging today. It therefore follows that the priest is to be a man of God and master of prayer. At the same time this obliges the priest to see to it that the community entrusted to his pastoral care is truly receptive so that no one belonging to it may feel faceless or the object of indifference. This is a responsibility that certainly does fall on all the faithful, but in particular on the priest, who is a man of communion. If he knows how to receive with esteem and respect each person who approaches him, appreciative of their value as persons, he will then generate a style of authentic charity that will become contagious and gradually extend to the entire community.

In addition to the desire for the eternal salvation of the faithful that beats in the heart of each priest, particularly important in rising to face and win the challenge of the sects and the new cults is a mature and complete catechesis, which calls for a special effort of the part of God's minister so all the faithful may really know the meaning of the Christian vocation

[191]    Cf. *ibid.*

and the Catholic faith. In this sense, "perhaps the simplest, most obvious and most urgent measure to be taken, the one which might also be the most effective, would be to make the most of the riches of the Christian spiritual heritage"[192].

In particular, the faithful must be educated to understanding in full the relationship between their specific vocation in Christ and belonging to his Church, which they must learn to love in a filial and tenacious way. All this will transpire if the priest, in his life and his ministry, avoids everything that could cause tepidity, frigidity or partial acceptance of the doctrine and norms of the Church. There is no doubt that for those who seek responses among the myriad of religious proposals, "the appeal of Christianity will be felt first of all in the witness of the members of the Church, in their trust, calm, patience and cheerfulness, and in their concrete love of neighbour, all the fruit of their faith nourished in authentic personal prayer"[193].

## Lights and Shadows of Ministerial Activity

48. It is most comforting to note today that priests of all ages and in the great majority carry out their sacred ministry with joyful commitment, often the result of silent heroism, working unto the extreme of their own strength without, at times, seeing the fruits of their labour.

As a result of this commitment they constitute today a living announcement of that divine grace, which, given freely at the moment of their Ordination, continues to give ever new strength for their ministry.

Along with these lights that illuminate the life of a priest, there are also shadows that tend to weaken its beauty and render the exercise of the ministry less credible: "In the world of today, with so many duties which people must undertake and

---

[192] PONTIFICAL COUNCIL FOR INTER-RELIGIOUS DIALOGUE, Document *Jesus Christ, Bearer of Living Water. Chritian Reflection on the "New Age"*, § 6.2 (3 February 2003): *EV* 22, 54-137.
[193] *Ibid.*

the great variety of problems vexing them and very often demanding a speedy solution, there is often ranger for those whose energies are divided by different activities. Priests are often perplexed and distracted by the very many obligations of their position may be anxiously enquiring how they can reduce to unity their interior life and their program of external activity"[194].

The pastoral ministry is a fascinating yet arduous endeavour open to misunderstanding and marginalisation, and especially today, subject to fatigue, pessimism, isolation, and at times solitude.

In order to rise to the challenges constantly posed by the secularlised mentality all around him, the priest must make every effort to reserve absolute primacy to the spiritual life, to being always with Christ, and to living pastoral charity with generosity, intensifying communion with all, and above all with other priests. As Benedict XVI recalled to priests: "The relationship with Christ, the personal colloquy with Christ, the personal dialogue with Christ is a fundamental pastoral priority in our work for the others! And prayer is not a marginal thing: it is the 'occupation' of the priest to pray, as representative of the people who do not know how to pray or do not find time to pray"[195].

## 2.2. Being with Christ in Prayer

*The Primacy of the Spiritual Life*

49. The priest as such was, so to speak, *conceived* in that long prayer during which our Lord Jesus spoke with the Father about his Apostles, and most certainly all those who down through the centuries would be made participants in his self-

---

[194]   ECUMENICAL COUNCIL VATICAN II, Decree *Presbyterorum Ordinis*, 14.
[195]   BENEDICT XVI, *Prayer Vigil on the Occasion of the Conclusion of the Year for Priests* (10 June 2010): *l.c.*, 397-406.

same mission (cf. *Lk* 6:12; *Jn* 17:15-20)[196]. The very prayer of Jesus in Gethsemane (cf. *Mt* 26:36-44) leading towards the priestly sacrifice of Golgotha manifests in a paradigmatic way "how our priesthood should be profoundly linked to prayer: rooted in prayer"[197].

Born of these prayers and called to renew in a sacramental and bloodless manner a Sacrifice inseparable from them, priests will keep their ministry alive with a spiritual life, to which they will give absolute pre-eminence, avoiding any neglect due to other activities.

Precisely in order to carry out his pastoral ministry in a fruitful manner, the priest needs to enter into a special and profound relationship with Christ the Good Shepherd, who alone remains the principal agent of any pastoral endeavour: "He [Christ] [...] remains always the principle and source of the unity of the life of priests. Therefore, priests will achieve the unity of their life by joining themselves with Christ in the recognition of the Father's will and in the gift of themselves to the flock entrusted to them. In this way, by adopting the role of the Good Shepherd they will find in the practice of pastoral charity itself the bond of priestly perfection which will reduce to unity their life and activity"[198].

*Means for the Spiritual Life*

50. In effect, evident among the grave contradictions of the relativistic culture is an authentic disintegration of the personality caused by a darkening of the truth about man. The risk of dualism in priestly life is always present.

This spiritual life must be incarnated in each priest through the liturgy, personal prayer, his style of life and the practice of the Christian virtues, which contribute to the fe-

---

[196]   Cf. BENEDICT XVI, *Homily at the Chrism Mass* (9 April 2009): *Insegnamenti* V/1 (2009), 578-583.

[197]   JOHN PAUL II, *Letter to Priests for Holy Thursday* (13 April 1987): *AAS* 79 (1987), 1285-1295.

[198]   ECUMENICAL COUNCIL VATICAN II, Decree *Presbyterorum Ordinis*, 14.

cundity of ministerial action. Conformation of self to Christ requires the priest to cultivate a climate of friendship with the Lord Jesus, living the experience of a personal encounter with Him, and placing himself at the service of the Church, His Body, which he will show he loves through the faithful and tireless fulfilment of the duties of the pastoral ministry[199].

It is therefore necessary that never lacking in the priest's life of prayer are to be the daily celebration of the Eucharist[200], with suitable preparation and ensuing thanksgiving; frequent confession[201] and spiritual direction already practiced in the seminary, and often even before that[202]; the complete and fervent celebration of the liturgy of the hours[203], which is a daily obligation for him[204]; examination of conscience[205]; the regular practice of mental prayer[206]; the *lectio divina*[207], prolonged mo-

---

[199]  Cf. *C.I.C.*, can. 276, § 2, 1°.

[200]  Cf. ECUMENICAL COUNCIL VATICAN II, Decree *Presbyterorum Ordinis* , 5; 18; JOHN PAUL II, Post-Synodal Apostolic Exhortation *Pastores dabo vobis*, 23; 26; 38; 46; 48; *C.I.C.*, cann. 246, § 1; 276, § 2, 2°.

[201]  Cf. ECUMENICAL COUNCIL VATICAN II, Decree *Presbyterorum Ordinis*, 5; 18; *C.I.C.*, cann. 246, § 4; 276, § 2, 5°; JOHN PAUL II, Post-Synodal Apostolic Exhortation *Pastores dabo vobis*, 26; 48.

[202]  Cf. ECUMENICAL COUNCIL VATICAN II, Decree *Presbyterorum Ordinis*, 18; *C.I.C.*, can. 239; JOHN PAUL II, Post-Synodal Apostolic Exhortation *Pastores dabo vobis*, 40; 50; 81.

[203]  Cf. ECUMENICAL COUNCIL VATICAN II, Decree *Presbyterorum Ordinis*, 18; *C.I.C.*, cann. 246, § 2; 276, § 2, 3°; JOHN PAUL II, Post-Synodal Apostolic Exhortation *Pastores dabo vobis*, 26; 72; CONGREGATION FOR DIVINE WORSHIP AND THE DISCIPLINE OF THE SACRAMENTS, Responses *Celebratio integra* to questions about the obligatory nature of the recital of the Liturgy of Hours (15 November 2000), in *Notitiae* 37 (2001), 190-194.

[204]  Cf. *C.I.C.* can. 1174, § 1.

[205]  ECUMENICAL COUNCIL VATICAN II, Decree *Presbyterorum Ordinis*, 18; JOHN PAUL II, Post-Synodal Apostolic Exhortation *Pastores dabo vobis*, 26; 37-38; 47; 51; 53; 72.

[206]  Cf. *C.I.C.*, can. 276, § 2, 5°.

[207]  Cf. ECUMENICAL COUNCIL VATICAN II, Decree *Presbyterorum Ordinis*, 4; 13; 18; JOHN PAUL II, Post-Synodal Apostolic Exhortation *Pastores dabo vobis*, 26; 47; 53; 70; 72.

ments of silence and colloquium, especially in periodical spiritual retreats and days of recollection[208]; the precious expressions of Marian devotion, such as the Rosary[209]; the *Via Crucis* and other pious exercises[210]; the fruitful reading of the lives of the saints[211]; etc. The proper and good use of time out of love for God and the Church will undoubtedly enable the priest to more easily maintain a solid life of prayer. Indeed, the priest, with the assistance of his spiritual director, is advised to make an effort to follow this plan of prayer that enables him to grow interiorily in a context where the manifold demands of life might often induce him to action for the sake of action, and to overlook the spiritual dimension.

Each year during the Chrism Mass on Holy Thursday, and as a sign of an enduring desire of fidelity, priests are to renew, in the presence of and together with the Bishop, the promises made at Ordination[212].

The care for the spiritual life that keeps the enemy of tepidity at bay must be felt as a joyful duty by the priest himself, but also as a right of the faithful who, consciously or unconsciously, seek in him *the man of God*, the counsellor, the mediator of peace, the faithful and prudent friend, the sure guide to confide in during more difficult moments in life in order to find comfort and assurance[213].

---

[208]   Cf. ECUMENICAL COUNCIL VATICAN II, Decree *Presbyterorum Ordinis*, 18; *C.I.C.*, can. 276, § 2, 4°; JOHN PAUL II, Post-Synodal Apostolic Exhortation *Pastores dabo vobis*, 80.

[209]   Cf. ECUMENICAL COUNCIL VATICAN II, Decree *Presbyterorum Ordinis*, 18; *C.I.C.*, cann. 246, § 3; 276, § 2, 5°. JOHN PAUL II, Post-Synodal Apostolic Exhortation *Pastores dabo vobis*, 36; 38; 45; 82.

[210]   Cf. ECUMENICAL COUNCIL VATICAN II, Decree *Presbyterorum Ordinis*, 18; JOHN PAUL II, Post-Synodal Apostolic Exhortation *Pastores dabo vobis*, 26; 37-38; 47; 51; 53; 72.

[211]   Cf. ECUMENICAL COUNCIL VATICAN II, Decree *Presbyterorum Ordinis*, 18.

[212]   Cf. JOHN PAUL II, *Letter to Priests for Holy Thursday 1979* (8 April 1979), 1: *l.c.*, 394; Post-Synodal Apostolic Exhortation *Pastores dabo vobis*, 80.

[213]   Cf . POSSIDIUS, *Vita Sancti Aurelii Augustini*, 31: PL 32, 63-66.

In the *Magisterium* of Benedict XVI there is a text of lofty significance regarding the battle against spiritual tepidity that must be waged also by those who are closer to the Lord because of the ministry: "No one is closer to his master than the servant who has access to the most private dimensions of his life. In this sense 'to serve' means closeness, it requires familiarity. This familiarity also bears a danger: when we continually encounter the sacred it risks becoming habitual for us. In this way, reverential fear is extinguished. Conditioned by all our habits we no longer perceive the great, new and surprising fact that he himself is present, speaks to us, gives himself to us. We must ceaselessly struggle against this becoming accustomed to the extraordinary reality, against the indifference of the heart, always recognising our insufficiency anew and the grace that there is in the fact that he consigned himself into our hands"[214].

### Imitating Christ in Prayer

51. Due to numerous duties stemming in large part from pastoral activity, the priest's life is now linked more so than ever before to a series of requests that could lead him to mounting *activism,* making him subject to a pace at times overwhelming and frenetic.

Not to be forgotten against this temptation is the first intention of Jesus, which was to call to his side Apostles so they "would remain with him" (*Mk* 3:14).

The Son of God himself wished to leave us testimony of his prayer. Indeed, quite frequently do the Gospels present Christ in prayer: in the revelation of his mission by the Father (cf. *Lk* 3:21-22), before the calling of the Apostles (cf. *Lk* 6:12), in giving thanks to God in the multiplication of the loaves of bread (cf. *Mt* 14:19; 15:36; *Mk* 6:41; 8:7; *Lk* 9:16; *Jn* 6:11), in the Transfiguration on the mountain (cf. *Lk* 9: 28-29), when he healed the deaf-mute (cf. *Mk* 7:34) and brought Laza-

---

[214] BENEDICT XVI, *Homily at the Chrism Mass* (20 March 2008): *Insegnamenti* IV/1 (2008), 442-446.

rus back to life (cf. *Jn* 11:41 ff.), before the confession of Peter (cf. *Lk* 9:18), when he taught the disciples how to pray (cf. *Lk* 11:1) and when they returned after completing their mission (cf. *Mt* 11:25 ff.; *Lk* 10:21 ff.), in the blessing of the children (cf. *Mt* 19:13) and on the prayer for Peter (cf. *Lk* 22:32), etc.

Everything in his daily activity issued forth from prayer. Thus did he retreat to the desert or on the mountain to pray (cf. *Mk* 1:35; 6:46; *Lk* 5:16; *Mt* 4:1; *Mt* 14:23), rose early (cf. *Mk* 1:35) or spent the entire night in prayer with God (cf. *Mt* 14:23.25; *Mk* 6:46.48; *Lk* 6:12).

Until the very end of his life, at the Last Supper (cf. *Jn* 17:1-26), in the agony of the garden (cf. *Mt* 26:36-44 par.) and on the Cross (cf. *Lk* 23:34.46; *Mt* 27:46; *Mk* 15:34), the divine Master demonstrated that prayer gave life to his Messianic ministry and his Paschal exodus. Risen from the dead, he lives forever and prays for us (cf. *Heb* 7:25)[215].

Therefore, the fundamental priority for each priest is his personal relationship with Christ through the abundance of moments of silence and prayer for cultivating and deepening his relationship with the living person of the Lord Jesus. Following the example of St. Joseph, the silence of the priest "manifests not an interior vacuum but, on the contrary, the fullness of the faith he bears in his heart and which guides his every thought and deed"[216]. A silence, which like that of the holy Patriarch "preserves the Word of God known through the Sacred Scriptures, constantly confronting it with the events in the life of Jesus; a silence woven with constant prayer, prayer of blessing of the Lord, adoration of his holy will, and unreserved entrustment to his providence[217].

In the communion of the holy Family of Nazareth the silence of Joseph was in perfect harmony with the recollection

---

[215]    Cf. *Institutio Generalis Liturgiae Horarum*, 3-4; *Catechism of the Catholic Church*, 2598-2606.

[216]    BENEDICT XVI, *Angelus* (18 December 2005): *Insegnamenti* I (2005), 1003.

[217]    *Ibid.*

of Mary, "the most perfect embodiment" of the obedience of the faith[218], who "kept all the 'great things' the Almighty had done and treasured them in her heart"[219].

In this way the faithful will see in the priest a man impassioned with Christ, bearing within himself the fire of His love; a man who knows he is loved by the Lord and abounds with love for his flock.

*Imitating the Church in Prayer*

52. In order to remain faithful to the commitment of "remaining with Christ" it is necessary for the priest to know how to imitate the Church in prayer.

In dispensing the Word of God, which he himself has received with joy, the priest is to remember the exhortation made by the Bishop on the day of his Ordination: "Therefore, making the Word the object of your continual reflection, always believe what you read, teach what you believe, and do in your life what you teach. In this way, through the doctrine which nourishes the People of God and with the upright witness of life you will be of comfort and support to them, you will become a builder of the temple of God, which is the Church". Likewise, regarding the celebration of the sacraments and in particular the Eucharist: "Be aware, then, of what you are doing, imitate what you do, and since you celebrate the mystery of the Lord's death and resurrection, bear the death of the Lord in your body and walk in the newness of life". Lastly, regarding the pastoral guidance of the People of God so he may lead them to the Father, "Therefore, never turn your face from Christ, the Good Shepherd, who has come not to be served, but to serve, and to seek and save those who are lost"[220].

---

[218]   *Catechism of the Catholic Church*, 144.
[219]   *Ibid.*, 2599; *Lk* 2:19.51.
[220]   *Pontificale Romanum, De ordinatione Episcopi, Presbyterorum et Diaconorum*, II, 151, *l.c.*, 87-88.

*Prayer as Communion*

53. Strengthened by the special bond with the Lord, the priest will know how to confront those moments when he might feel alone among men, resolutely renewing his being and remaining with Christ in the Eucharist, the real place of the presence of his Lord.

Like Christ, who while alone was always with the Father (cf. *Lk* 3:21; *Mk* 1:35), the priest as well must be a man who, in recollection, silence and solitude, finds communion with God[221], so he can say with St. Ambrose: "I am never less alone than as when I seem to be alone"[222].

Alongside the Lord the priest will find the strength and the means to bring men closer to God, to ignite their faith and inspire both commitment and sharing.

## 2.3. Pastoral Charity

*Manifestation of the Charity of Christ*

54. Intimately connected to the Eucharist, pastoral charity constitutes the internal and dynamic principle capable of uniting the priest's multiple and diverse pastoral activities and bringing men to the life of Grace.

The ministerial activity must be a manifestation of the charity of Christ, whose bearing and conduct the priest will know how to project, and this unto the ultimate donation of self for the good of the flock entrusted to him[223]. In a special way will he be close to those who suffer, the little ones, chil-

---

[221]    Cf. ECUMENICAL COUNCIL VATICAN II, Decree *Presbyterorum Ordinis*, 18; SYNOD OF BISHOPS, Document on the Ministerial priesthood *Ultimis temporibus* (30 November 1971), II, I, 3: *l.c.*, 913-915; JOHN PAUL II, Post-Synodal Apostolic Exhortation *Pastores dabo vobis*, 46-47; *General Audience* (2 June 1993), 3: *Insegnamenti* XVI/1, 1389.

[222]    "Numquam enim minus solus sum, quam cum solus esse videor": *Epist. 33* (Maur. 49), 1: *CSEL* 82, 229.

[223]    Cf. ECUMENICAL COUNCIL VATICAN II, Decree *Presbyterorum Ordinis*, 14; JOHN PAUL II, Post-Synodal Apostolic Exhortation *Pastores dabo vobis*, 23.

dren, outcasts and the poor, bringing the Good Shepherd's love and compassion to all.

The assimilation of the pastoral charity of Christ in order to make it become a form of his own life is a goal that requires the priest to live an intense Eucharistic life, as well as continuous efforts and sacrifices, since this charity cannot be improvised, knows no breaks, and cannot be considered as attained once for all. The minister of Christ will feel it his obligation to live and bear witness to this reality always and everywhere, also when he may have be relieved of pastoral responsibilities for reasons of age.

*Beyond Functionalism*

55. Pastoral charity runs the risk, especially nowadays, of being emptied of its meaning by what is called *functionalism*. In fact, it is not rare to perceive, also in some priests, the influence of a mentality which tends erroneously to reduce the ministerial priesthood to functional aspects alone. "Doing" as a priest, providing individual services and guaranteeing the performance of certain tasks would be the essence of priestly existence as such. But the priest does not just do a "job", after which he would be free for his own pursuits: such a reductive conception of the identity and ministry of priests runs the risk of pushing a priest towards an abyss, which is often filled with forms of life not consonant with his ministry.

The priest, who knows he is a minister of Christ and the Church, and works as a man impassioned with Christ with all the forces of his life at the service of God and men, will find in prayer, study and spiritual reading the force necessary to surmount this danger as well[224].

## 2.4. Obedience

*The Basis of Obedience*

56. Obedience is a virtue of primary importance and is

---

[224]    Cf. *C.I.C.*, can. 279, § 1.

closely united with charity. As the Servant of God Paul VI teaches, in "pastoral charity" it is possible to transcend "the relationship of juridical obedience, so obedience itself may be willing, sincere and secure"[225]. The very sacrifice of Jesus on the Cross acquired salvific value and significance through his obedience and fidelity to the Father's will. He was "obedient unto death, and death on a cross" (*Ph* 2:8). The Letter to the Hebrews also underscores that Jesus "learned obedience from the things He suffered" (*Heb* 5:8). It could therefore be said that obedience to the Father is at the very heart of the Priesthood of Christ.

Just like that of Christ, the priest's obedience expresses total and joyful readiness to do God's will. This is why the priest recognises that this Will also becomes evident in the indications of legitimate superiors. Readiness towards the latter in this regard is to be understood as true enactment of personal liberty, a consequence of a choice ceaselessly matured before God in prayer. The virtue of obedience, intrinsically requested by the sacrament and the hierarchical structure of the Church, is explicitly promised by the cleric, first in the rite of ordination to the diaconate, and then in the rite of ordination to the priesthood. With this promise the priest strengthens his will in communion, thereby entering into the dynamics of the obedience of Christ, who became obedient Servant unto death on the Cross (cf. *Phi* 2:7-8)[226].

Highlighted in contemporary culture is the importance of the subjectivity and autonomy of each person as intrinsic to his dignity. In itself positive in nature, when this reality is rendered absolute and claimed outside its proper context it assumes a negative significance[227]. This can also become manifest in ecclesial circles, and in the very life of the priest if and when the

---

[225]   PAUL VI, Encyclical Letter *Sacerdotalis caelibatus*, 93.

[226]   Cf. *Ibid.*, 15; JOHN PAUL II, Post-Synodal Apostolic Exhortation *Pastores dabo vobis*, 27.

[227]   Cf. JOHN PAUL II, Encyclical Letter *Veritatis splendor* (6 August 1993), 31; 32; 106: *AAS* 85 (1993), 1158-1159; 1159-1160; 1216.

activities he performs for the good of the community were to be reduced to the level of a purely subjective fact.

In reality, the priest, by the very nature of his ministry, is at the service of Christ and the Church. Therefore, he must be disposed to accepting all that is justly indicated by his Superiors, and in particular, if he is not legitimately impeded, he must accept and faithfully perform the office committed to him by his Ordinary[228].

The Decree *Presbyterorum Ordinis* describes the foundations of the obedience of priests beginning from the divine work to which they are called and then illustrates the framework of this obedience:

- The mystery of the Church: "The priestly ministry, given that it is the ministry of the Church herself, can only be fulfilled in the hierarchical union of the whole body of the Church"[229];

- Christian fraternity: "pastoral charity urges priests to act within this communion and by obedience to dedicate their own will to the service of God and their fellow-Christians, accepting and carrying out in the spirit of faith the commands and suggestions of the Supreme Pontiff and of their bishop and other superiors, and gladly spending themselves in whatever office is entrusted to them, even the humbler and poorer. By acting in this way they preserve and strengthen the indispensable unity with their brothers in the ministry and especially those whom the Lord has appointed the visible rulers of the Church, and working for the building up of the Body of Christ, which grows 'by what every joint supplies'"[230].

*Hierarchical Obedience*

57. The priest has "a special obligation to show reverence and obedience to the Supreme Pontiff and to his Ordinary"[231].

---

[228]  Cf. *C.I.C.*, can. 274, §2.
[229]  ECUMENICAL COUNCIL VATICAN II, Decree *Presbyterorum Ordinis*, 15.
[230]  *Ibid.*
[231]  Cf. *C.I.C.*, can. 273.

By virtue of belonging to a determined presbyterate he is charged with the service of a particular Church, whose principle and foundation of unity is the Bishop[232], who has all the ordinary, proper and immediate authority over it necessary for the exercise of his pastoral office[233]. The hierarchical subordination required by the sacrament of Holy Orders has its ecclesiological-structural enactment in reference to one's Bishop and the Roman Pontiff, who holds the primacy (*principatus*) of ordinary power over all the particular Churches[234].

The obligation to follow the *Magisterium* in matters of faith and morals is intrinsically linked to all the functions the priest must perform in the Church[235]. Dissent in this area is to be considered grave insofar as it leads to scandal and confusion among the faithful. The appeal to disobedience, especially regarding the definitive *Magisterium* of the Church, is not a way to renew the Church[236]. Its inexhaustible vivacity can only issue forth from following the Master, obedient unto the cross, in whose mission priests collaborate "with the joy of the faith, the radicality of obedience, the dynamism of hope, and the force of love"[237].

No one is more aware than the priest that the Church needs norms, whose purpose is to ensure suitable protection to the gifts of the Holy Spirit entrusted to the Church. In fact, since its hierarchical and organic structure is visible, the exer-

---

[232]    Cf. ECUMENICAL COUNCIL VATICAN II, Dogmatic Constitution *Lumen gentium*, 23.

[233]    Cf. *ibid.*, 27; *C.I.C.*, can. 381, § 1.

[234]    Cf. ECUMENICAL COUNCIL VATICAN II, Decree *Christus Dominus*, 2; Dogmatic Constitution *Lumen gentium*, 22; *C.I.C.*, can. 333, § 1.

[235]    Cf. On the *Professio fidei*, *C.I.C*, can. 833 and CONGREGATION FOR THE DOCTRINE OF THE FAITH, Formula to be used for the profession of faith and the oath of fidelity in assuming an office to be exercised in the name of the Church, with a doctrinal Note illustrating the conclusive part of the *Professio fidei* (29 June 1998): *AAS* 90 (1998), 542-551.

[236]    Cf. BENEDICT XVI, *Homily at the Chrism Mass* (5 April 2012): "L'Osservatore Romano", 6 April 2012, 7.

[237]    *Ibid.*

cise of the functions divinely entrusted to it, especially those relative to the guidance and celebration of the sacraments, must be suitably organised[238].

Insofar as a minister of Christ and his Church, the priest generously takes upon himself the duty to comply faithfully with each and every norm, avoiding those forms of partial compliance, according to subjective criteria, which create division and have damaging effects upon the lay faithful and public opinion. In fact, "canonical norms demand observance by their very nature" and require "that what is commanded by the head be observed by the members"[239].

In obeying the constituted authority, the priest, furthermore, will enhance mutual charity within the priesthood, as well as that unity whose foundation is to be found in truth.

*Authority Exercised with Charity*

58. In order for the observance of obedience to be facilitated and able to nourish ecclesial communion, those constituted in positions of authority – Ordinaries, religious Superiors, Moderators of Societies of apostolic life –, in addition to offering the necessary and constant personal example, must exercise their institutional charism with charity, both anticipating and requesting, in due times and ways, adhesion to each norm in the *ambit of the Magisterium and discipline*[240].

This adhesion is a source of liberty since it stimulates and does not hamper the mature spontaneity of the priest, who will be in a position to assume a serene and even-minded pastoral position, creating the harmony in which personal genius merges in a higher unity.

---

[238]    Cf. JOHN PAUL II, Apostolic Constitution *Sacrae disciplinae leges* (25 January 1983): *AAS* 75 (1983), Pars II, XIII; *Address to the Participants at the International Symposium "Ius in vita et in missione Ecclesiae"* (23 April 1993): "L'Osservatore Romano", 25 April 1993, 4.

[239]    Cf. JOHN PAUL II, Apostolic Constitution *Sacrae disciplinae leges* (25 January 1983): *l.c.*, Pars II, XIII.

[240]    Cf. *C.I.C.*, cann. 392; 619.

## Respect for Liturgical Norms

59. Worthy of emphasis among the various aspects of the question felt the most today is convinced love and respect for liturgical norms.

The liturgy is the exercise of the priestly office of Jesus Christ[241], "the summit toward which the activity of the Church is directed; it is also the fount from which all her power flows"[242]. It constitutes an ambit in which the priest must have particular awareness of being a minister, a servant, and having to faithfully obey the Church. "The ordering and guidance of the sacred liturgy depends solely upon the authority of the Church, namely, that of the Apostolic See and, as provided by law, that of the diocesan Bishop"[243]. The priest, therefore, may not add, remove, or change anything in the liturgy on his own initiative[244].

This is especially true for the celebration of the sacraments, which are acts of Christ and the Church *par excellence,* and which the priest administers in the person of Christ the Head and in the name of the Church for the good of the faithful[245]. The latter have a true right to participate in liturgical celebrations as the Church, so wills and not according to the personal likes of a particular minister, nor according to unapproved and unusual rites, which are expressions of specific groups that tend to isolate themselves from the universality of the People of God.

## Unity in Pastoral Planning

60. In the exercise of their ministry it is necessary for

---

[241] Cf. ECUMENICAL COUNCIL VATICAN II, Constitution *Sacrosanctum Concilium*, 7.

[242] *Ibid.*, 10.

[243] *C.I.C.*, can. 838.

[244] Cf. ECUMENICAL COUNCIL VATICAN II, Constitution *Sacrosanctum Concilium*, 22.

[245] Cf. *C.I.C.*, can. 846, § 1.

priests not only to participate in the definition of the pastoral plans which the Bishop determines with the collaboration of the Council of Priests[246], but also ensure harmony between them and practical activities in their respective community.

Far from being mortified, the sapiential creativity and spirit of initiative proper to the maturity of priests may be suitably enhanced for the full advantage of pastoral effectiveness. Embarking upon separate avenues in this realm may in fact lead to a weakening of the work of evangelisation itself.

## The Importance and Obligatory Nature of Ecclesiastical Attire

61. In a secularised and basically materialistic society where the external signs of sacred and supernatural realities tend to disappear, deeply felt is the need for the priest – man of God, dispenser of his mysteries – to be recognisable in the eyes of the community by his attire as well, and this as an unequivocal sign of his dedication and identity as holder of a public ministry[247]. The priest must be recognisable above all through his conduct, but also by his attire, which renders visible to all the faithful, and to each person[248], his identity and his belonging to God and to the Church.

Clerical attire is the external sign of an interior reality: "Indeed, the priest no longer belongs to himself but, because of the sacramental seal he has received (cf. *Catechism of the Catholic Church,* nn. 1563, 1582), is the 'property' of God. The priest's 'belonging to Another', must become recognisable to all, through a transparent witness. [...] In the way of thinking,

---

[246] Cf. SACRED CONGREGATION FOR THE CLERGY, Circular Letter *Omnes Christifideles* (25 January 1973), 9: *EV* 5, 1207-1208.

[247] JOHN PAUL II, *Letter to the Cardinal Vicar of Rome* (8 September 1982): *Insegnamenti* V/2 (1982), 847-849.

[248] Cf. PAUL VI, *Allocutions to the Clergy* (17 February 1969; 17 February 1972; 10 February 1978): *AAS* 61 (1969), 190; 64 (1972), 223; 70 (1978), 191; JOHN PAUL II, *Letter to Priests for Holy Thursday 1979* (8 April 1979), 7: *l.c.,* 403-405; *Allocutions to the Clergy* (9 November 1978; 19 April 1979): *Insegnamenti* I (1978), 116; II (1979), 929.

speaking, and judging events of the world, of serving and loving, of relating to people, also in his habits, the priest must draw prophetic power from his sacramental belonging"[249].

For this reason the priest, like the transitory deacon, must[250]:

a) wear either the cassock "or suitable ecclesiastical dress, in accordance with the norms established by the Episcopal Conference and legitimate local customs"[251]; when other than the cassock, attire must be different from the way laypersons dress and consonant with the dignity and sanctity of the minister; the style and the colour are to be determined by the Conference of Bishops;

b) because of their incoherence with the spirit of this discipline, contrary practices are bereft of the rationality necessary for them to become legitimate customs[252] and must be absolutely eliminated by the competent authority[253].

Outside of specific exceptional cases, the non use of ecclesiastical attire may manifest a weak sense of one's identity as a pastor dedicated entirely to the service of the Church[254].

Moreover, in its form, colour and dignity the cassock is most opportune, because it clearly distinguishes priests from laymen and makes people understand the scared nature of their ministry, reminding the priest himself that forever and at each

---

[249]    BENEDICT XVI, *Address to the Participants at the Theological Conference Organised by the Congregation for the Clergy* (12 March 2010): l.c., 241.

[250]    Cf. PONTIFICAL COUNCIL FOR LEGISLATIVE TEXTS, *Clarifications Regarding the Binding Nature of Article 66 of the Directory on the Ministry and Life of Priests* (22 October 1994): "Communicationes" 27 (1995), 192-194.

[251]    *C.I.C.*, can. 284.

[252]    Cf. *ibid.*, can. 24, § 2.

[253]    Cf. PAUL VI, Motu Proprio *Ecclesiae Sanctae*, I, 25, § 2; SACRED CONGREGATION FOR BISHOPS, Circular Letter to all the Pontifical Representatives *Per venire incontro* (27 January 1976): *EV* 5, 1162-1163; SACRED CONGREGATION FOR CATHOLIC EDUCATION, Circular Letter *The Document* (6 January 1980): "L'Osservatore Romano" supplement, 12 April 1980.

[254]    Cf. PAUL VI, *General Audience* (17 September 1969); *Allocution to the Clergy* (1 March 1973): *Insegnamenti* VII (1969), 1065; XI (1973), 176.

moment he is a priest ordained to serve, teach, guide, and sanctify souls mainly through the celebration of the sacraments and the preaching of the Word of God. Wearing ecclesiastical attire is also a safeguard for poverty and chastity.

## 2.5. Preaching the Word

*Fidelity to the Word*

62. Christ entrusted to the Apostles and the Church the mission of preaching the Good News to all men.

To transmit the faith is to prepare a people for the Lord, revealing, proclaiming and deepening the Christian vocation, which is the calling God addresses to each man in showing him the mystery of salvation, and at the same time the place he is to occupy in reference to that mystery as an adopted child[255]. This dual aspect is succinctly brought to light in the Symbol of Faith, one of the most authoritative expressions with which the Church has always responded to the call of God[256].

The priestly ministry is therefore faced with two requirements. First of all there is the missionary nature of the transmission of the faith. The ministry of the Word cannot be abstract or distant with respect to the life people live; on the contrary, it must make direct reference to the life of man, each man, and hence must enter into the most pressing questions being posed to the human conscience.

On the other hand there is the need for authenticity and conformity with the faith of the Church, the guardian of the truths concerning God and man. This must be done with a sense of extreme responsibility, in the awareness that it is a matter of utmost importance insofar as at stake is the life of man and the sense of his existence.

For an effective ministry of the Word, and ever conscious of this context, the priest will reserve primacy to the witness of

[255]    Cf. ECUMENICAL COUNCIL VATICAN II, Dogmatic Constitution *Dei Verbum*, 5; *Catechism of the Catholic Church*, 1-2, 142.
[256]    Cf. *ibid.*, 150-152, 185-187.

life, which reveals the power of God's love and renders his word persuasive. Moreover, he will not neglect the explicit preaching of the mystery of Christ to believers, to non Christians and to non believers; catechesis, which is the ordinary and organic exposition of the doctrine of the Church; the application of the revealed truth to the solution of concrete cases[257].

The awareness of the absolute need to "remain" faithful to and anchored in the Word of God and Tradition in order to be true disciples of Christ and know the truth (cf. *Jn* 8:31-32) has always accompanied the history of the priestly spirituality, and was also reiterated in an authoritative manner by the Second Vatican Ecumenical Council[258]. Hence, most useful is the "longstanding practice of the *lectio divina*, or 'spiritual reading' of Sacred Scripture. This consists in spending considerable time on a biblical text, reading it and rereading it, almost 'ruminating it' as the Fathers say, and, we might say, squeezing out all its 'juice' so it may nourish meditation and contemplation, and be able to irrigate concrete life much like sap"[259].

Above all for contemporary society marked as it is in many countries by theoretical and practical materialism, subjectivism and cultural relativism, it is necessary for the Gospel to be presented as "the power of God for the salvation of everyone who believes" (*Rm* 1:16). Priests, recalling that "the faith comes from what is preached, and what is preached comes from the word of Christ" (*Rm* 10:17), will devote their every energy to correspond to this mission, which is primary in their ministry. Indeed, they are not only witnesses, but heralds and transmitters of the faith[260].

Carried out in the hierarchical communion, this ministry

---

[257]   Cf. JOHN PAUL II, *General Audience* (21 April 1993), 6: *Insegnamenti* XVI/1 (1993), 936-947.
[258]   Cf. ECUMENICAL COUNCIL VATICAN II, Dogmatic Constitution *Dei Verbum*, 25.
[259]   BENEDICT XVI, *Angelus* (6 November 2005): *Insegnamenti* I/1 (2005), 759-762.
[260]   Cf. *C.I.C.*, cann. 757; 762; 776.

empowers them to express the Catholic faith with authority and bear witness to the faith in the name of the Church. In effect, the People of God "is formed into one in the first place by the Word of the living God, which everyone has the right to hear from the mouths of priests"[261].

In order to be authentic the Word must be transmitted without duplicity and without any falsification, but rather manifesting with frankness the truth before God (cf. *2Cor* 4:2). With responsible maturity the priest will avoid falsifying, reducing, distorting or diluting the contents of the divine message. His role, in fact, "is not to teach his own wisdom but the Word of God, and urgently invite all men to conversion and holiness"[262]. "Consequently, his words, his choices and his behaviour must increasingly become a reflection, proclamation and witness of the Gospel; only if he 'abides' in the word will the priest become a perfect disciple of the Lord. Only then then will he know the truth and be set truly free"[263].

Preaching, therefore, can not be reduced to the presentation of one's own thoughts, the manifestation of personal experience, or to simple explanations of a psychological[264], sociological or philanthropic nature; nor can it indulge excessively on the allure of rhetoric so often found in mass communication. It is a matter of proclaiming a Word not at our disposal insofar as it has been given to the Church so the Church herself may protect, penetrate and transmit it in all fidelity[265]. Nonetheless, it is necessary for the priest to prepare his preaching in a suitable manner through prayer, serious and up-

---

[261]   ECUMENICAL COUNCIL VATICAN II, Decree *Presbyterorum Ordinis*, 4.

[262]   *Ibid.*; cf. JOHN PAUL II, Post-Synodal Apostolic Exhortation *Pastores dabo vobis*, 26.

[263]   BENEDICT XVI, Post-Synodal Apostolic Exhortation *Verbum Domini* (30 Septemebr 2010), 80: *AAS* 102 (2012), 751-752.

[264]   Cf. JOHN PAUL II, *General Audience* (12 May 1993): *Insegnamenti* XVI/1 (1993), 1194-1204.

[265]   Cf. ECUMENICAL COUNCIL VATICAN II, Dogmatic Constitution *Dei Verbum*, 10; JOHN PAUL II, *General Audience* (12 May 1993): *l.c.*, 1194-1204.

dated study, and the commitment to apply what he says concretely to the conditions of those to whom he preaches. In particular, as Benedict XVI recalled, "during the course of the liturgical year it is appropriate to offer the faithful, prudently and on the basis of the three-year lectionary, 'thematic' homilies treating the great themes of the Christian faith, on the basis of what has been authoritatively proposed by the *Magisterium* in the four "pillars" of the *Catechism of the Catholic Church* and the recent *Compendium,* namely, the profession of faith, the celebration of the Christian mystery, life in Christ and Christian prayer[266]. Thus will homilies and catechesis, etc., be of true help to the faithful for the bettering their life of relationship with God and others.

## Word and Life

63. The awareness of the mission to announce the Gospel as an instrument of God and the Holy Spirit is to become increasingly concrete in pastoral terms so the priest may vivify in the light of the Word of God the diverse situations and settings in which he carries out his ministry.

In order to be effective and credible it is therefore important that the priest – within the perspective of the faith and his ministry – be familiar in a constructive critical sense with the ideologies, language, cultural intricacies and typologies diffused through the mass media, and which to a great extent condition the ways people think.

Stirred by the Apostle who exclaimed: "Woe to me if I do not preach the Gospel!" (*1Cor* 9:16), he must know how to use all those means of communication placed at his disposal by the sciences and modern technology.

Certainly, not all depends on such means or human skills, since divine grace can attain its effect independently of the workings of man. In the plan of God, however, the preaching

---

[266]     BENEDICT XVI, Post-Synodal Apostolic Exhortation *Sacramentum caritatis,* 46.

of the Word is customarily the preferred channel for the transmission of the faith and the evangelising mission.

For those who today are outside or far removed from the proclamation of Christ the priest will consider particularly urgent and timely the dramatic question: "How are they to invoke Him in whom they have not believed? How are they to believe him whom they have not heard? And how are they to hear if no one preaches him?" (*Rm* 10:14).

In order to respond to such questions the priest must feel personally engaged in cultivating the Sacred Scriptures in a special way through the study of sound exegesis, mainly patristic, and through meditation in keeping with the various methods supported by the spiritual tradition of the Church in order to obtain an understanding moved by love[267]. It is particularly important to teach the cultivation of this personal relationship with the Word of God already during the years in the seminary, where candidates to the priesthood are called to study the Scriptures in order to become increasingly "aware of the mystery of divine revelation and foster an attitude of prayerful response to the Lord who speaks. Conversely, an authentic life of prayer cannot fail to nurture in the candidate's heart a desire for greater knowledge of the God who has revealed himself in his word as infinite love"[268].

64. The priest is to feel it his duty to reserve special attention to the remote and immediate preparation of the liturgical homily and its contents, echoing the liturgical readings, especially the Gospel, the equilibrium between exposition and application, pedagogy, and techniques of presentation – including good diction – ever respectful of the dignity of the act being performed and the listeners[269]. In particular, "generic and abstract homilies which obscure the directness of God's word should be avoided, as well as useless digressions which risk

---

[267]   Cf. St. Thomas Aquinas, *Summa theologiae*, I, q. 43, a. 5.

[268]   Benedict XVI, Post-Synodal Apostolic Exhortation *Verbum Domini*, 82.

[269]   Cf. *C.I.C.*, can. 769.

drawing greater attention to the preacher than to the heart of the Gospel message. The faithful should be able to perceive clearly that the preacher has a compelling desire to present Christ, who must stand at the centre of every homily"[270].

## Word and Catechesis

65. Nowadays when spreading in many surroundings is a religious illiteracy where the fundamental elements of the faith are increasingly less known, catechesis proves to be a basic part of the Church's mission of evangelisation, since it is a preferred instrument in the teaching and maturation of the faith[271].

The priest, as a collaborator of the Bishop and duly mandated by him, bears the responsibility to animate, coordinate and direct the catechetical activity of the community entrusted to him. It is important for him to be able to integrate this activity into an organic project of evangelisation, guaranteeing above all the communion of the catechesis of his community with the person of the Bishop, the particular Church and the universal Church[272].

In particular he must know how to inspire the correct and opportune responsibility and collaboration regarding catechises with both the members of Institutes of Consecrated Life and Societies of apostolic life, and suitably prepared lay faithful[273], manifesting towards them his recognition and esteem for their work in catechesis.

He is to devote special care to the initial and continuing formation of catechists, associations and movements. Insofar as possible, the priest is to be the *catechist of the catechists,* forming together with them a true community of the Lord serving

---

[270]   BENEDICT XVI, Post-Synodal Apostolic Exhortation *Verbum Domini*, 59.

[271]   Cf. JOHN PAUL II, Apostolic Exhortation *Catechesi tradendae* (16 October 1979), 18: *AAS* 71 (1979), 1291-1292.

[272]   Cf. *C.I.C.*, can. 768.

[273]   Cf. *C.I.C.*, cann. 528, §1 and 776.

as a point of reference for those receiving Christian instruction. Thus he will teach them that the service of the ministry of teaching must be based on the Word of Jesus Christ and not on personal theories or opinions: it is "the faith of the Church of whom we are servants"[274].

Master[275] and educator of the faith[276], the priest will ensure that catechesis is a privileged part of Christian education in families, in religious education, in the formation of apostolic movements, etc., and that it is addressed to all the categories of the faithful: children, adolescents, adults, the elderly. Moreover, he will know how to transmit catechetical teaching with the use of all those didactic aids and instruments, as well as means of communication that may be effective so the faithful, in a manner suited to their disposition, ability, age, and practical conditions of life, may be able to learn the Christian doctrine in full and put it into practice in the most fitting way[277].

To this end, the priest will have as his main point of reference is to be the *Catechism of the Catholic Church* and its *Compendium*. In fact, these texts constitute the sound and authentic norm for the teaching of the Church[278], and their reading and study is therefore to be encouraged. They must always be the sure and irreplaceable basis for teaching "the fundamental content of the faith that receives its systematic and organic synthesis in the *Catechism of the Catholic Church*"[279]. As His Holiness Benedict XVI recalled, in the *Catechism* "we see the wealth of teaching that the Church has received, safeguarded and proposed in her two thousand years of history. From Sacred

---

[274]     BENEDICT XVI, *Homily at the Chrism Mass* (5 April 2012): *l.c.*, 7.

[275]     Cf. ECUMENICAL COUNCIL VATICAN II, Decree *Presbyterorum Ordinis*, 9.

[276]     Cf. *ibid.*, 6.

[277]     Cf. *C.I.C.*, can. 779.

[278]     Cf. JOHN PAUL II, Apostolic Constitution *Fidei depositum* (11 October 1992): *AAS* 86 (1992), 113-118.

[279]     BENEDICT XVI, Apostolic Letter issued Motu Proprio *Porta fidei* (11 October 2011), 11: *AAS* 103 (2011), 730.

Scripture to the Fathers of the Church, from theological masters to the saints across the centuries, the *Catechism* provides a permanent record of the many ways in which the Church has meditated on the faith and made progress in doctrine so as to offer certitude to believers in their lives of faith"[280].

## 2.6. The Sacrament of the Eucharist

*The Eucharistic Mystery*

66. While the service of the Word is the fundamental element of the priestly ministry, its heart and vital centre is undoubtedly the Eucharist, which is above all the real presence in time of the one and eternal sacrifice of Christ[281].

Sacramental memorial of the death and resurrection of Christ, real and efficacious representation of the singular redeeming Sacrifice, source and apex of the Christian life and all evangelisation[282], the Eucharist is the beginning, means and end of the priestly ministry, since "all ecclesiastical ministries and works of the apostolate are bound up with the Holy Eucharist and are directed towards it"[283]. Consecrated in order to perpetuate the Holy Sacrifice, the priest thus manifests his identity in the most evident manner[284].

In fact, there is an intimate connection among the centrality of the Eucharist, pastoral charity and the unity of the life of

---

[280]    *Ibid.*

[281]    Cf. JOHN PAUL II, *General Audience* (12 May 1993), 3: *l.c.*, 1195-1196.

[282]    Cf. ECUMENICAL COUNCIL VATICAN II, Decree *Presbyterorum Ordinis*, 5; BENEDICT XVI, Post-Synodal Apostolic Exhortation *Sacramentum caritatis* (22 February 2007), 78; 84-88: *l.c.*, 165; 169-173.

[283]    *Ibid.*

[284]    "Sacerdos habet duos actus: unum principalem, supra corpus Christi verum; et alium secundarium, supra corpus Christi mysticum. Secundus autem actus dependet a primo, sed non convertitur" (ST. THOMAS, *Summa theologiae, Suppl.*, q. 36, a. 2, ad 1).

the priest[285], who therein finds decisive indications for the way to holiness to which he has been specifically called.

If the priest lends to Christ, the Most Eternal High Priest, his intelligence, his will, his voice and his hands so through his ministry he may offer to the Father the sacramental sacrifice of redemption, he is to embrace the dispositions of the Master and, like him, live as a *gift* for his brothers. He is therefore to learn to unite himself intimately to the offering, placing on the altar of the sacrifice his whole life as a revealing sign of God's gratuitous and prevenient love.

## *Celebrating the Eucharist Well*

67. The priest is called to celebrate the Holy Eucharistic Sacrifice, to meditate constantly on what it means and transform his life into a Eucharist, which becomes manifest in love for daily sacrifice, especially in fulfilling the duties and offices proper to his state. Love for the cross leads the priest to become himself an offering pleasing to the Father through Christ (cf. *Rm* 12:1). Loving the Cross in a hedonistic society is a scandal, but from a perspective of faith it is the fount of interior life. The priest must preach the redemptive value of the cross with his style of life.

It is necessary to evoke the irreplaceable value for the priest of the daily celebration of the Holy Mass – the "source and summit"[286] of the priestly life – even if it should not be

---

[285]  Cf. ECUMENICAL COUNCIL VATICAN II, Decree *Presbyterorum Ordinis*, 5; 13; ST. JUSTIN, *Apologia* I, 67: *PG* 6, 429-432; ST. AUGUSTINE, *In Iohannis Evangelium Tractatus*, 26, 13-15: *CCL* 36, 266-268; BENEDICT XVI, Post-Synodal Apostolic Exhortaiton *Sacramentum caritatis*, 80; CONGREGATION FOR DIVINE WORSHIP AND THE DISCIPLINE OF THE SACRAMENTS, Instruction *Redemptionis Sacramentum* on certain things that must be observed and avoided regarding the Most Holy Eucharist (25 March 2004), 110: *AAS* 96 (2004), 581.

[286]  ECUMENICAL COUNCIL VATICAN II, Dogmatic Constitution *Lumen gentium*, 11; cf. also, Decree *Presbyterorum Ordinis*, 18.

possible to have the faithful present[287]. In this regard Benedict XVI teaches: "To this end I join the Synod Fathers in recommending 'the daily celebration of the Holy Mass, even when the faithful are not present'. This recommendation is consistent with the objectively infinite value of every celebration of the Eucharist, and is motivated by its unique spiritual fruitfulness. If celebrated in a faith-filled and attentive way, the Holy Mass is formative in the deepest sense of the word, since it fosters the priest's configuration to Christ and strengthens him in his vocation"[288].

He is to live the celebration of the Eucharist as the core moment of his day and his daily ministry, the fruit of sincere desire and occasion for a deep and effective encounter with Christ. In the Eucharist the priest learns to give himself each day, not only in moments of great difficulty, but also in minor daily setbacks. This learning experience is reflected in love in preparing himself for the celebration of the Holy Sacrifice and living it in piety without haste, ever attentive to the liturgical norms and the rubrics so the faithful may in this manner perceive an authentic catechesis[289].

In a civilisation ever more sensitive to communication through signs and images, the priest is to allocate due attention to everything that can exalt the decorum and sacredness of the Eucharistic celebration. It is important that in such celebrations proper attention is focused on the appropriateness and cleanliness of the place, the architecture of the altar and the tabernacle[290], the nobility of the sacred vessels, the vest-

---

[287]    Cf. *C.I.C.*, can. 904.

[288]    BENEDICT XVI, Post-Synodal Apostolic Exhortation *Sacramentum caritatis*, 80.

[289]    Cf. *Ibid.*, 64: *l.c.*, 152-154.

[290]    Cf. ECUMENICAL COUNCIL VATICAN II, Constitution *Sacrosanctum Concilium*, 128; JOHN PAUL II, Encyclical Letter *Ecclesia de Eucharistia*, 49-50; BENEDICT XVI, Post-Synodal Apostolic Exhortation *Sacramentum caritatis*, 80.

ments[291], the hymns[292], the music[293], the sacred silence[294], and the use of incense during more solemn celebrations, etc., repeating that loving act of Mary towards the Lord, when "she took a pound of very costly ointment, pure nard, and with it anointed the feet of Jesus, wiping them with her hair; the house was full of the scent of the ointment" (*Jn* 12:3). These are all elements that can contribute to a better participation in the Eucharistic celebration. In fact, limited attention to the symbolic aspects of the liturgy, and even more so things such as carelessness and haste, superficiality and disorder empty its meaning and detract from its function of fostering growth in the faith[295]. The priests who fail to celebrate the Holy Mass well reveal the weakness of their faith and do not educate others to the faith. Conversely, celebrating the Holy Mass well constitutes an initial important catechesis on the Holy Sacrifice.

In a special way the liturgical norms must be respected with generous fidelity during the celebration of the Eucharist. "The liturgical norms for the celebration of the Eucharist are to be observed with great fidelity. These norms are a concrete expression of the authentically ecclesial nature of the Eucharist; this is their deepest meaning. Liturgy is never anyone's private property, be it of the celebrant or of the community in which the mysteries are celebrated. [...] Our time, too, calls for

---

[291]    Cf. ECUMENICAL COUNCIL VATICAN II, Constitution *Sacrosanctum Concilium*, 122-124; CONGREGATION FOR DIVINE WORSHIP AND THE DISCIPLINE OF THE SACRAMENTS, Instruction *Redemptionis Sacramentum* (25 March 2004), 121-128: *l.c.*, 583-585.

[292]    Cf. ECUMENICAL COUNCIL VATICAN II, Constitution *Sacrosanctum Concilium*, 112, 114, 116; JOHN PAUL II, Encyclical Letter *Ecclesia de Eucharistia* (17 April 2003), 49: *l.c.*, 465-466; BENEDICT XVI, Post-Synodal Apostolic Exhortation *Sacramentum caritatis*, 42.

[293]    Cf. ECUMENICAL COUNCIL VATICAN II, Constitution *Sacrosanctum Concilium*, 120.

[294]    Cf. *ibid.*, 30; BENEDICT XVI, Post-Synodal Apostolic Exhortation *Sacramentum caritatis*, 55.

[295]    Cf. *C.I.C.*, can. 899, § 3.

a renewed awareness and appreciation of liturgical norms as a reflection of, and a witness to, the one universal Church made present in every celebration of the Eucharist. Priests who faithfully celebrate Mass according to the liturgical norms, and communities which conform to those norms, quietly but eloquently demonstrate their love for the Church"[296].

Therefore, the priest, while placing at the service of the Eucharistic celebration all his talents to make it come alive in the participation of the faithful, must abide by the rite stipulated in the liturgical books approved by the competent authority, without adding, removing or changing anything at all[297]. Thus his celebrating truly becomes a celebration of and with the Church: he does not do "something of his own", but is with the Church in dialogue with God. This also promotes adequate active participation on the part of the faithful in the sacred liturgy: "The *ars celebrandi* is the best way to ensure the *actuosa participatio*. The *ars celebrandi* is the fruit of faithful adherence to the liturgical norms in all their richness; indeed, for two thousand years this way of celebrating has sustained the faith life of all believers, called to take part in the celebration as the People of God, a royal priesthood, a holy nation" (cf. *1P* 2:4-5.9)[298].

All Ordinaries, Superiors of Institutes of consecrated life and Moderators of Societies of apostolic life bear the grave responsibility, besides for being first in example, of exercising vigilance so that the liturgical norms regarding the celebration

---

[296]  JOHN PAUL II, Encyclical Letter *Ecclesia de Eucharistia*, 52; Cf. CONGREGATION FOR DIVINE WORSHIP AND THE DISCIPLINE OF THE SACRAMENTS, Instruction *Redemptionis Sacramentum* (25 March 2004): *l.c.*, 549-601.

[297]  Cf. ECUMENICAL COUNCIL VATICAN II, Constitution *Sacrosanctum Concilium*, 22; *C.I.C.*, can. 846, § 1; BENEDICT XVI, Post-Synodal Apostolic Exhortation *Sacramentum caritatis*, 40.

[298]  BENEDICT XVI, Post-Synodal Apostolic Exhortation *Sacramentum caritatis*, 38.

of the Eucharist are faithfully observed at all times by all and in all places.

Priests who celebrate or concelebrate are obliged to wear the sacred vestments prescribed by the liturgical norms[299].

*Eucharistic Adoration*

68. The centrality of the Eucharist must appear not only in the worthy and deeply felt celebration of the Sacrifice, but also in frequent adoration of the Sacrament of the Altar so the priest may be seen as a model for the flock also in devout attention and assiduous meditation in the presence of the Lord in the tabernacle. It is hoped that the priests entrusted with the guidance of communities would dedicate long periods of time to community adoration – for example, every Thursday, the days of prayer for vocations, etc. – and reserve to the Blessed Sacrament of the Altar, also outside Holy Mass, attention and honours superior to any other rite and act. "Faith and love for the Eucharist may not permit the presence of Christ in the Tabernacle to remain alone"[300]. Inspired by the example of their pastors' faith, the faithful will seek occasions throughout the week to go to church and adore our Lord present in the Tabernacle.

A privileged moment of Eucharistic adoration could be during the celebration of the Liturgy of the Hours, which con-

---

[299] Cf. *C.I.C.*, can. 929; *Institutio Generalis Missalis Romani* (2002), 81; 298; SACRED CONGREGATION FOR DIVINE WORSHIP AND THE DISCIPLINE OF THE SACRAMENTS, Instruction *Liturgicae instaurationes* (5 September 1970), 8: *AAS* 62 (1979), 701; Instruction *Redemptionis Sacramentum* (25 March 2004), 121-128: *l.c.*, 583-585.

[300] JOHN PAUL II, *General Audience* (9 June 1993), 6: *Insegnamenti* XVI/1 (1993), 1469-1461; cf. Post-Synodal Apostolic Exhortation *Pastores dabo vobis*, 48; *Catechism of the Catholic Church*, 1418; JOHN PAUL II, Encyclical Letter *Ecclesia de Eucharistia*, 25; CONGREGATION FOR DIVINE WORSHIP AND THE DISCIPLINE OF THE SACRAMENTS Instruction *Redemptionis Sacramentum*, 13; BENEDICT XVI, Post-Synodal Apostolic Exhortation *Sacramentum caritatis*, 67-68.

stitutes a prolongation during the day of the sacrifice of praise and thanksgiving, whose centre and sacramental fount is the Holy Mass. The Liturgy of the Hours, in which the priest united to Christ is the voice of the Church for the world, will be celebrated, also in a communitarian form, in such a way as to be "the interpreter and vehicle of the universal voice chanting the glory of God and asking for the salvation of man"[301].

Exemplary solemnity of this celebration will be reserved to the canonical Chapters.

Therefore, whether it be in communitarian or individual form, the Liturgy of the Hours is always to be celebrated with love and the yearning for reparation, without falling into a simple "duty" to be performed in a mechanical fashion as a mere and hasty reading without paying the necessary attention to the meaning of what is being read.

## Mass Intentions

69. "The Eucharist is a sacrifice because it *re-presents* (makes present) the sacrifice of the cross, because it is its *memorial* and because it *applies* its fruit"[302]. Each Eucharistic celebration makes present the one, perfect and definitive sacrifice of Christ, who saved the world on the Cross once for all. The Eucharist is celebrated first of all for the glory of God and in thanksgiving for the salvation of mankind. According to a very ancient tradition, the faithful request the priest to celebrate Mass so that it "may be offered in reparation for the sins of the living and the dead, and to obtain spiritual or temporal benefits from God"[303]. "It is earnestly recommended to priests that they celebrate Mass for the intentions of Christ's faithful"[304].

---

[301]   JOHN PAUL II, *General Audience* (2 June 1993), 5: *l.c.*, 1390-1391; cf. ECUMENICAL COUNCIL VATICAN II, Constitution *Sacrosanctum Concilium*, 99-100.

[302]   *Catechism of the Catholic Church*, 1366.

[303]   *Ibid.*, 1414; cf. *C.I.C.*, can. 901.

[304]   Cf. *C.I.C.*, can. 945, § 2.

In order to participate in their own way in the Sacrifice of the Lord with the gift not only of themselves, but also a part of what they possess, the faithful associate an offering, usually a sum of money, to the intention for which they wish a Holy Mass to be applied. In no way is this a form of *remuneration,* since the Eucharistic Sacrifice is absolutely gratuitous. "Urged by their religious and ecclesial sense, the faithful, with a view to a more active participation in the Eucharistic celebration, wish to add their personal offering, thereby contributing to the needs of the Church and in particular to the support of her ministers[305]. The offering for the celebration of Holy Masses is to be considered 'an excellent form' of almsgiving[306].

This practice is "not only approved, but also encouraged by the Church, which considers it a sort of sign of the union of baptised persons with Christ, as well as of the priest with the faithful for whom he carries out his ministry"[307]. Priests are therefore to encourage it with a suitable catechesis, explaining its spiritual sense and fecundity to the faithful. They themselves will take special care in celebrating the Eucharist with the full awareness that, in Christ and with Christ, they are the intercessors before God, not only to apply the Sacrifice of the Cross for the salvation of humanity, but also to present to divine benevolence the particular intention entrusted to them. This is one of the excellent ways for the lay faithful to participate actively in the celebration of the memorial of the Lord.

Priests are also to be convinced that "since this matter directly touches the august sacrament, any albeit minimum shadow of profit or simony would cause scandal"[308]. The Church

---

[305] PAUL VI, Motu Proprio *Firma in traditione* (13 June 1974): *AAS* 66 (1974), 308.
[306] CONGREGATION FOR THE CLERGY, Decree *Mos iugiter* (22 February 1991), art. 7: *AAS* 83 (1991), 446.
[307] PAUL VI, Motu Proprio *Firma in traditione* (13 June 1974): *l.c.*, 308.
[308] CONGREGATION FOR THE CLERGY, Decree *Mos iugiter* (22 February 1991): *l.c.*, 443-446.

has therefore issued precise rules in this regard[309] and punishes with a just penalty "a person who unlawfully traffics in Mass offerings"[310]. Each priest who accepts the engagement to celebrate a Holy Mass according to the intentions of the person making the offering must comply therewith pursuant to the obligation of justice, applying as many Masses as there are intentions[311].

It is not licit for a priest to ask for an amount higher than what has been determined by decree issued by the legitimate authority, or, if that sum does not exist, a sum corresponding to the customary practice in use in the diocese. Nonetheless, he may accept an offering less than the established amount, and even a higher amount if such an offering is spontaneously made[312].

"Each priest must accurately record the Masses which he has accepted to celebrate and those which he has in fact celebrated"[313]. The parish priest and the rector of a church must record them in a special register[314].

A priest may only accept offerings for Masses which may be celebrated within the year[315]. "Priests who receive offerings for a large number of Masses to be applied to special intentions [...], far from turning them down and thereby frustrating the pious wishes of those making the offering and dissuading them from their good intention, are to transfer them to other priests (cf. *C.I.C.* can. 955) or to their own Ordinary (cf. *C.I.C.* can. 956)"[316].

---

[309] Cf. *C.I.C.*, cann. 945-958.
[310] *Ibid.*, can. 1385.
[311] Cf. *ibid.*, cann. 948-949; 199, 5°.
[312] Cf. *C.I.C.*, can. 952.
[313] *Ibid.*, can. 955, 4.
[314] Cf. *ibid.*, can. 958, § 1.
[315] Cf *ibid.*, can. 953.
[316] CONGREGATION FOR THE CLERGY, Decree *Mos iugiter* (22 February 1991), art. 5, § 1: *l.c.*, 443-446.

"If persons making an offering are explicitly consulted beforehand and freely consent for their offerings to be accumulated with others in a single offering, their wishes may be satisfied with a single Holy mass celebrated according to a single 'collective' intention. In this case the day, place and time of the celebration of the Mass are to be publicly indicated, and such Masses may not be celebrated more than twice a week"[317]. Were it to be used excessively, this waver to Canon law in force would constitute a reprehensible abuse[318].

If the priest celebrates more than once on the same day he may retain for himself the offering for only one Mass and transmits the others for purposes prescribed by the Ordinary[319].

Each parish priest "is bound on each Sunday and holyday of obligation to apply the Mass for the people entrusted to him"[320].

## 2.7. The Sacrament of Penance

*The Ministry of Reconciliation*

70. The Gift of the Risen One to the Apostles is the Holy Spirit for the remission of sins: "Receive the Holy Spirit. Whose sins you shall forgive, they are forgiven them; and whose sins you shall retain, they are retained" (*Jn* 20:21-23). Christ entrusted the sacramental work of Reconciliation of man with God exclusively to his Apostles, and to those who succeed them in the same mission[321]. By the will of Christ, priests are the only ministers of the sacrament of Reconcilia-

---

[317]  *Ibid.*, art. 2, §§ 1-2, 443-446.

[318]  Cf. *ibid.*, art. 2, § 3, 443-446.

[319]  Cf. *C.I.C.*, can. 951.

[320]  *Ibid.*, can. 534, § 1.

[321]  Cf. ECUMENICAL COUNCIL OF TRENT, Sessio VI, *De Iustificatione*, c. 14; sess. XIV, *De Poenitentia*, c. 1, 2, 5-7, can. 10; Sessio XXIII, *De Ordine*, c. 1; ECUMENICAL COUNCIL VATICAN II, Decree *Presbyterorum Ordinis*, 2, 5; *C.I.C.*, can. 965.

tion. Like Christ, they are invited to call sinners to conversion and bring them back to the Father through the judgment of mercy.

Sacramental Reconciliation restores the friendship with God the Father and with all his children in his family which is the Church, and which is thereby rejuvenated and edified in all its dimensions: universal, diocesan and parochial[322].

Despite the sad fact of the loss of the sense of sin, which is so broadly present in the cultures of our time, the priest must practice the ministry of the formation of consciences, forgiveness and peace with dedication and joyfulness.

It is therefore necessary for him to be able to identify himself in a certain sense with this sacrament, and, assuming the disposition of Christ, mercifully bend over wounded humanity as a Good Samaritan, projecting the Christian newness of the medicinal dimension of penance, which is in view of healing and pardon[323].

## *Dedication to the Ministry of Reconciliation*

71. Because of both his office[324] and his priestly ordination, the priest is to dedicate time – also with established days and times – and energies to hearing the confessions of the faithful[325], who, as experience demonstrates, willing go to receive this sacrament where they know and see priests available. Moreover, not to be overlooked is the possibility of facilitating recourse to the sacrament of Reconciliation and Penance on the part of individual faithful during the celebration of the Holy Mass[326]. This applies everywhere, but especially for ca-

---

[322]    Cf. *Catechism of the Catholic Church*, 1443-1445.

[323]    Cf. *C.I.C.*, cann. 966, § 1; 978, § 1; 981; JOHN PAUL II, *Address to the Apostolic Penitentiary* (27 March 1993): *Insegnamenti* XVI/1 (1993), 761-766.

[324]    Cf. *C.I.C.*, can. 986.

[325]    Cf. JOHN PAUL II, Apostolic Letter issued Motu Proprio *Misericordia Dei* (7 April 2002), 1-2: *l.c.*, 455.

[326]    "Local Ordinaries, and parish priests and rectors of churches and shrines, must periodically verify that the greatest possible provision is in fact

thedral churches, churches in more frequented areas, centres of spirituality and sanctuaries, where fraternal and responsible collaboration with religious priests and elderly priests is possible[327].

We cannot forget that "the faithful and generous readiness of priests to hear confessions, following the example of great saints of history, from St. John Mary Vianney to St. John Bosco, from St. Josemaría Escrivá to St. Pio di Pietralcina, from St. Joseph Cafasso to St. Leopold Mandić, is an indication for all of us of how the confessional can be a real 'place' of sanctification"[328].

Every priest is to abide by the ecclesial norm that defends and promotes the value of individual confession with the integral accusation of sins in direct colloquy with the confessor[329]. "Individual and integral confession and absolution are the sole ordinary means by which the faithful, conscious of grave sin, are reconciled with God and the Church", and therefore, "all those of whom it is required by virtue of their ministry in the care of souls are obliged to ensure that the confessions of the faithful entrusted to them are heard"[330]. Sacramental absolutions given in a collective form without having observed the

being made for the faithful to confess their sins. It is particularly recommended that in places of worship confessors be visibly present at the advertised times, that these times be adapted to the real circumstances of penitents, and that confessions be especially available before Masses, and even during Mass if there are other priests available, in order to meet the needs of the faithful": JOHN PAUL II Apostolic Letter *Misericordia Dei* (2 May 2002), 2: *l.c.*, 455.

[327] Cf. CONGREGATION FOR THE CLERGY, *Circular Letter to the Rectors of Shrines* (15 August 2011): "L'Osservatore Romano", 12 August 2011, 7.

[328] BENEDICT XVI, *Address to the participants at the Course Organised by the Apostolic Penitentiary* (25 March 2011): "L'Osservatore Romano", 26 March 2011, 7.

[329] Cf. *C.I.C.*, can. 960; JOHN PAUL II, Encyclical Letter *Redemptor hominis*, 20: *AAS* 64 (1979), 257-324; Apostolic Letter *Misericordia Dei*, 3.

[330] JOHN PAUL II, Apostolic Letter *Misericordia Dei*, 1.

established norms are undoubtedly to be considered a grave abuse[331].

Regarding the place for confessions, the relative norms are established by the Episcopal Conference, "nonetheless guaranteeing that confessionals with a fixed grating between the penitent and the confessor are always located in a visible manner so the faithful who so desire may freely make use thereof"[332]. The confessor will be able to enlighten the conscience of the penitent with words which, however brief, will be suited to his concrete situation, and thus enhance a renewed personal orientation toward conversion and have a profound impact on his spiritual journey, also through the imposition of an opportune penance[333]. In this manner confession could be lived also as a moment of spiritual direction.

In any case, the priest is to know how to maintain the celebration of Reconciliation on a sacramental level, stimulating sorrow for sins and trust in grace, etc., and at the same time overcoming the danger of reducing it to a purely psychological exercise or a merely formalistic act.

Moreover, this becomes clear in faithfully following the norms in force regarding the place for confessions, which

---

[331] The use of community confession and absolution is reserved solely to extraordinary cases and under the required conditions contemplated by dispositions in force: cf. *C.I.C.*, canons 961-963; PAUL VI, *Allocution* (20 March 1978): *AAS* 70 (1978), 328-332; JOHN PAUL II, *Allocution* (30 January 1981): *AAS* 73 (1981), 201-204; Post-Synodal Apostolic Exhortation *Reconciliatio et paenitentia* (2 December 1984), 33: *AAS* 77 (1985), 270; Apostolic Letter *Misericordia Dei*, 4-5.

[332] *C.I.C.*, can. 964, §2. Moreover, the minister of the sacrament, for just cause and the case of necessity excluded, may legitimately decide, even if the penitent requests otherwise, that the sacramental confession is to be received in a confessional fitted with a fixed grille. (Cf. PONTIFICAL COUNCIL FOR LEGISLATIVE TEXTS, *Responsio ad propositum dubium: de loco excipiendi sacramentales confessiones: AAS* 90 [1998], 711).

[333] Cf. *C.I.C.*, cann. 978, § 1; 981.

must not be heard "outside the confessional, except for just cause"[334].

## The Necessity of Confession

72. Like all the faithful, the priest also needs to confess his sins and weaknesses. He is the first to know that the practice of this sacrament strengthens him in faith and charity towards God and his brothers.

In order to be in the best condition to reveal effectively the beauty of Penance, it is essential for the minister of the sacrament to offer personal witness by preceding the other faithful in living the experience of pardon. This also constitutes the first condition for restoring the pastoral value of the sacrament of Reconciliation: in frequent confession the priest learns how to understand others, and – following the example of the Saints – is urged to place them at the centre of [...] pastoral concerns [335]. In this sense it is something good for the faithful to know and see that their priests also go to confession on a regular basis[336]. "The whole of priestly existence suffers an inexorable decline if by negligence or for some other reason a priest fails to receive the sacrament of penance at regular intervals and in a spirit of genuine faith and devotion. If a priest were no longer to go to confession or properly confess his sins, his priestly being and his priestly action would feel its effects very soon and this would also be noticed by the community of which he was the pastor"[337].

---

[334]    *Ibid.*, can. 964; JOHN PAUL II, Apostolic Letter *Misericordia Dei*, 9.

[335]    BENEDICT XVI, *Letter Establishing the Year for Priests on the Occasion of the 150th Anniversary of the "Dies natalis" of John Mary Vianney*, 16 June 2009: *l.c.*, 569-579.

[336]    Cf. *C.I.C.*, can. 276, § 2, 5°; ECUMENICAL COUNCIL VATICAN II, Decree *Presbyterorum Ordinis*, 18.

[337]    JOHN PAUL II, Post-Synodal Apostolic Exhortation *Reconciliatio et paenitentia*, 31; Post-Synodal Apostolic Exhortation *Pastores dabo vobis*, 26.

73. Along with the sacrament of Reconciliation the priest will not fail to exercise the ministry of *spiritual direction*[338]. The rediscovery and extension of this practice, also at times outside the administration of Penance, is of great benefit for the Church in these times[339]. The generous and active attitude of priests in practicing it also constitutes an important occasion for identifying and sustaining vocations to the priesthood and to the various forms of consecrated life.

In order to contribute to the improvement of their spirituality it is necessary for priests to practice spiritual direction with respect to themselves, because "with the assistance of accompaniment or spiritual counsel [...] it is easier to discern the action of the Holy Spirit in each person's life"[340]. By placing the formation of their soul in the hands of a wise confrere – the instrument of the Holy Spirit – they will develop, as of their first steps in the ministry, their awareness of the importance of not journeying in solitude along the ways of the spiritual life and pastoral commitment. In making use of this efficacious means of formation so well tried and proven in the Church, priests are to exercise complete liberty in choosing the person who may guide them.

## 2.8. The Liturgy of the Hours

74. A fundamental way for the priest to be in the presence of the Lord is the Liturgy of the Hours. In this liturgy we pray

---

[338]  Cf. BENEDICT XVI, *Message to Cardinal James Francis Stafford, Major Penitentiary, and the Participants at the XX Edition of the Course for the Internal Forum Organised by the Apostolic Penitentiary* (12 March 2009): *l.c.*, 374-377; CONGREGATION FOR THE CLERGY, *The Priest, Minister of Divine Mercy. Material for Confessors and Spiritual Directors* (9 March 2011), 64-134: *l.c.*, 28-53.

[339]  Cf. JOHN PAUL II, Post-Synodal Apostolic Exhortation *Reconciliatio et paenitentia*, 32.

[340]  CONGREGATION FOR THE CLERGY, *The Priest, Minister of Divine Mercy. Material for Confessors and Spiritual Directors* (9 March 2011), 98: *l.c.*, 39; cf. *ibid.* 110-111: *l.c.*, 42-43.

as men in need of dialogue with God, giving voice to and standing in for all those who perhaps do not know, do not want or do not find the time to pray.

The Second Vatican Ecumenical Council recalls that the faithful "who take part in the divine office are not only performing a duty for the Church, they are also sharing in what is the greatest honour for Christ's Bride; for by offering these praises to God they are standing before God's throne in the name of the Church, their Mother"[341]. This prayer is "the voice of the Bride herself addressed to her Bridegroom. It is the very prayer which Christ himself together with his Body addresses to the Father"[342]. In this sense the priest prolongs the prayer of Christ the Priest and brings it into the present.

75. The daily obligation to pray the Breviary (the Liturgy of the Hours) is also one of the solemn commitments undertaken in ordination to the diaconate in public form, which may not be omitted without grave cause. It is an obligation of love that is to be attended to under all circumstances, including during times of vacation. The priest "is obliged to pray all the Hours daily"[343], that is to say, Morning Prayer (Lauds) and Evening Prayer (Vespers), as well as the Office of Readings, at least one of the parts of Daytime Prayer, and Night Prayer (Compline).

76. Required for priests to be able to deepen the meaning of the Liturgy of the Hours is "not only harmonising the voice with the praying heart, but also a deeper 'understanding of the liturgy and of the Bible, espcially of the Psalms'"[344]. It is

---

[341]   ECUMENICAL COUNCIL VATICAN II, Constitution *Sacrosanctum Concilium*, 85.

[342]   *Ibid.*, 84.

[343]   BENEDICT XVI, Post-Synodal Apostolic Exhortation *Verbum Domini*, 62; cf. *Institutio Generalis Liturgiae Horarum*, 29; *C.I.C.*, cann. 276, §3; 1174, §1.

[344]   *Catechism of the Catholic Church*, 1176, citing ECUMENICAL COUNCIL VATICAN II, Constitution *Sacrosanctum Concilium*, 90.

therefore necessary to interiorise the divine Word, be attentive to what the Lord is telling 'me' with this Word, then listen to the commentary of the Fathers of the Church or the Second Vatican Ecumenical Council, deepen the life of the Saints and also the words of the Pontiff in the second Reading of the Office of Readings, and pray with this grand invocation that are the Psalms, with which we become one with the prayer of the Church. "To the degree we have interiorised this structure, understood this structure, assimilated the words of the Liturgy, we can enter into this interior consonance and thereby speak not only with God as indivudals, but enter into the 'we' of the praying Church. And in that way we also transform our 'I' by entering into the 'we' of the Church, enriching, expanding this 'I', praying with the Church, with the words of the Church, being truly in colloquy with God"[345]. More than reciting the Breviary it is a matter of fostering a disposition to listen, and also to live "the experience of silence"[346]. In fact, the Word can be pronounced and heard only in silence. At the same time, however, the priest knows that our time does not really favour recollection. Many times we have the impression that people are almost afraid of detaching themselves even for a moment from the instruments of mass communication[347]. This is why the priest must discover anew the sense of recollection and interior quietness "in order to receive in his heart the full resonence of the voice of the Holy Spirit and to unite personal prayer more closely with the Word of God and with the public voice of the Church[348]; he must increasingly interiorise his own nature as intercessor[349]. With the Eucharst, to which he is

---

[345]     BENEDICT XVI, *Meeting with the Priests of the Diocese of Albano*, Castel Gandolfo (31 August 2006): *Insegnamenti* II/2 (2006), 163-179.

[346]     JOHN PAUL II, Apostolic Letter *Spiritus et Sponsa*, 13: *AAS* 96 (2004), 425.

[347]     Cf. BENEDICT XVI, Post-Synodal Apostolic Exhortation *Verbum Domini*, 66.

[348]     *Institutio Generalis Liturgiae Horarum*, 202.

[349]     Cf. *Catechism of the Catholic Church*, 2634-2636.

"ordained", the priest becomes the intercessor qualified to bring before God with utmost simplicity of heart (*simpliciter*) questions confronting his fellow brothers. In his speech on the 30th anniversary of *Presbyterorum Ordinis* Pope John Paul II recalled: "The priestly identity is a question of fidelity to Christ and to the people of God to whom we are sent. The priestly conscience is not limited to something personal. It is a reality constantly examined and felt by men, because the priest is "taken" from among men and placed in order to intervene in their relations with God. [...] Since the priest is a mediator between God and men, numerous are those who turn to him asking for his prayers. In a certain sense, prayer 'creates' the priest, especially as a pastor. At the same time each priest 'creates himself' thanks to prayer. I have in mind the marvelous prayer of the Breviary, the *Officium Divinum*, in which the Church at large, through its ministers, prays with Christ"[350].

## 2.9. Guide of the Community

*Priest for the Community*

77. In addition to the requirements already examined, the priest is called to come to terms with another aspect of his ministry. This aspect has to do with attending to the life of the community entrusted to his care, which is expressed above all in his testimony of charity.

Pastor of the community – in the likeness of Christ, the Good Shepherd, who offers his whole life for the Church –, the priest exists and lives for it; prays, studies, works and sacrifices himself for it; is prepared to give his life for it, loving it like Christ, pouring out upon it all his love and considera-

---

[350] JOHN PAUL II, *Address to the Participants of the International Symposium on the Occasion of the XXX Anniversary of the Promulgation of the Conciliar Decree Presbyterorum Ordinis*, 27 October 1995, n. 5.

tion[351], lavishing it with all his strength and unlimited time to render it, in the image of the Church, the Bride of Christ, ever more beautiful and worthy of the benevolence of the Father and the love of the Holy Spirit.

This spousal dimension of the life of a priest as pastor will enable him to guide his community, serving all and each and all of its members with dedication, illuminating their consciences with the light of the revealed truth, authoritatively safeguarding the evangelical authenticity of the Christian life, correcting errors, forgiving, healing wounds, consoling afflictions, and fostering fraternity[352].

In addition to guaranteeing an ever more transparent and efficacious witness of charity, these forms of caring attention will also manifest the profound communion that must come to be between the priest and his community as a prolongation and present day enactment of the communion with God, with Christ and with the Church[353]. In imitation of Jesus, the priest is not called to be served, but to serve (cf. *Mt* 20:28). He must be constantly warned against the temptation, with a view to personal gains, to make abusive use of the great respect and deference the faithful show towards the priesthood and the Church.

---

[351]    Cf. JOHN PAUL II, Post-Synodal Apostolic Exhortation *Pastores dabo vobis*, 22-23; cf. Apostolic Letter *Mulieris dignitatem* (15 August 1988), 26: *AAS* 80 (1988), 1715-1716.

[352]    Cf. ECUMENICAL COUNCIL VATICAN II, Decree *Presbyterorum Ordinis*, 6; *C.I.C.*, can. 529, § 1.

[353]    ST. JOHN CHRYSOSTOM, *De sacerdotio*, III, 6: *PG* 48, 643-644: "The spiritual birth of souls is entrusted to priests: they bring souls to the life of grace through baptism; through them we put on Christ, we are buried with the Son of God and we become members of his Body (cf. *Rm* 6:1; *Gal* 3:27). Therefore, we should not only respect the priest more than princes or kings, but esteem him more than we do our parents. Indeed, our parents have begotten us through blood and by the will of the flesh (cf. *Jn* 1:13); while the priests have brought us to life as sons of God; they are the instruments of our joyful rebirth, of our freedom and of our adoption into the order of grace".

*To Listen with the Church*

78. In order to be a good guide of his People, the priest is also to be attentive to the signs of the times; from those that have to do with the universal Church and its journey in the history of man, to those closest to the concrete situation of a particular community.

This discernment calls for constant and correct updating in the study of the sacred sciences with reference to diverse theological and pastoral problems, and the exercise of a wise reflection on the social, cultural and scientific data characteristic of our present day and age.

In carrying out their ministry, priests are to know how to translate these demands into a constant and sincere attitude of *being of one mind with the Church,* and thus will always work in the bond of communion with the Pope, the Bishops, his confreres in the priesthood, deacons, the faithful consecrated through the profession of the evangelical counsels, and all the faithful.

Priest are to show fervent love for the Church, which is the mother of our Christian existence, and live the joy of ecclesial belonging as a precious form of witness for the entire People of God.

Moreover, they will not fail to request, in the legitimate ways and taking into due consideration the skills of each person, the cooperation of the consecrated faithful and other faithful in the exercise of their activity.

## 2.10. Priestly Celibacy

*The Steadfast Will of the Church*

79. Convinced of the profound theological and pastoral motives upholding the relationship between celibacy and the priesthood, and enlightened by the witness that today as well confirms its spiritual and evangelical validity in the lives of so many priests, the Second Vatican Ecumenical Council and later Pontifical *Magisterium* of the Church have repeatedly reiterated

"the firm will to maintain the law which requires celibacy freely chosen and perpetual for candidates to priestly Ordination in the Latin rite"[354].

Celibacy, in fact, is a joyful gift which the Church has received and wishes to retain, convinced that it is a good for itself and for the world.

*Theological and Spiritual Motivations for Celibacy*

80. Like any evangelical value, celibacy as well must be lived as a gift of divine mercy, a liberating development, a special witness of radicalism in the following of Christ, and a sign of the eschatological reality: "Celibacy is an anticipation rendered possible by the grace of the Lord, who 'pulls' us to himself towards the world of the resurrection; again and again does he invite us to transcend ourselves in this present, towards the true present of the future, which becomes present today"[355].

"Not all can understand it, but only those to whom it has been given. For there are eunuchs who were born so from their mothers' womb; and there are eunuchs who were made so by men; and there are eunuchs who have made themselves so for the Kingdom of heaven. He that can understand, let him understand" (*Mt* 19:10-12)[356]. Celibacy reveals itself to be correspondence in love on the part of a person, who, leaving "father and mother, follows Jesus the good shepherd in an apostolic communion, in the service of the People of God"[357].

In order to live with love and generosity the gift received, from the very beginning of his seminary formation it is particu-

---

[354]    JOHN PAUL II, Post-Synodal Apostolic Exhortation *Pastores dabo vobis*, 29; cf. ECUMENICAL COUNCIL VATICAN II, Decree *Presbyterorum Ordinis*, 16; PAUL VI, Encyclical Letter *Sacerdotalis caelibatus*, 14; *C.I.C.*, can. 277, § 1.

[355]    BENEDICT XVI, *Prayer Vigil on the Occasion of the Conclusion of the Year for Priests* (10 June 2010): *l.c.*, 397-406.

[356]    Cf. JOHN PAUL II, Encyclical Letter *Veritatis splendor* (6 August 1993), 22: *l.c.*, 1150-1151.

[357]    JOHN PAUL II, Post-Synodal Appostolic Exhortation *Pastores dabo vobis*, 29.

larly important for the priest to understand the theological dimension and the spiritual motivation of the ecclesial discipline on celibacy[358]. As a gift and particular charism of God, this demands the observance of perfect and perpetual continence for the Kingdom of heaven so the sacred ministers may more easily adhere to Christ with an undivided heart and dedicate themselves more freely to the service of God and man[359]: "Celibacy sets the whole man on a higher level and makes an effective contribution to his perfection"[360]. Even before the subject expresses his will to be so disposed, the ecclesiastical discipline manifests the will of the Church, and its ultimate reason is to be found in the intimate bond celibacy has with sacred Ordination, which configures the priest to Jesus Christ, Head and Spouse of the Church[361].

The Letter to the Ephesians closely relates the priestly oblation of Christ (cf. 5:25) with the sanctification of the Church (cf. 5:26) loved with a spousal love. Sacramentally inserted into this priesthood of Christ's excusive love for the Church, his faithful Bride, the priest expresses this love with his commitment of celibacy, which also becomes a wellspring for pastoral effectiveness.

Celibacy, therefore, is not an external effect brought to bear on the priestly ministry, nor can it be considered simple an institution laid down by law, also because he who receives the sacrament of Orders does so in all conscience and with full

---

[358] Cf. ECUMENICAL COUNCIL VATICAN II, Decree *Optatam totius*, 10; *C.I.C.*, can. 247, § 1; SACRED CONGREGATION FOR CATHOLIC EDUCATION, *Ratio Fundamentalis Institutionis Sacerdotalis* (19 marzo 1985), 48; *Educative Orientations for Formation to Priestly Celibacy* (11 April 1974), 16: *EV* 5 (1974-1976), 200-201.

[359] Cf. ECUMENICAL COUNCIL VATICAN II, Decree *Presbyterorum Ordinis*, 16; JOHN PAUL II, *Letter to Priests for Holy Thursday 1979* (8 April 1979), 8: *l.c.*, 405-409; Post-Synodal Apostolic Exhortation *Pastores dabo vobis*, 29; *C.I.C.*, can. 277, § 1.

[360] PAUL VI, Encyclical Letter *Sacerdotalis caelibatus*, 55.

[361] Cf. ECUMENICAL COUNCIL VATICAN II, Decree *Presbyterorum Ordinis*, 16; PAUL VI, Encyclical Letter *Sacerdotalis caelibatus*, 14.

liberty[362] after years of preparation, deep reflection and assiduous prayer. Together with the resolute conviction that Christ grants him this *gift* for the good of the Church and the service of others, the priest takes it upon himself for his whole life, strengthening this willingness in the promise already made during Ordination to the diaconate[363].

For these reasons, ecclesiastical law on one hand confirms the charism of celibacy, showing how it is in intimate connection with the sacred ministry in the dual dimension of relationship to Christ and to the Church; on the other hand it safeguards the liberty of those who embrace it[364]. Consecrated to Christ in a new and excellent way[365], the priest must therefore be well aware that he has received a gift from God, which, sanctioned in its turn by a precise juridical bond, gives rise to the moral obligation of observance. Freely assumed, this bond is theological and moral in nature before being juridical, and is the sign of that spousal reality coming to be in sacramental Ordination.

Through the gift of celibacy the priest also acquires that spiritual yet real fatherhood which is universal in dimension and assumes concrete expression particularly towards the community entrusted to him[366]. "These are children of his spirit, people entrusted to his solicitude by the Good Shepherd. These people are many, more numerous than an ordinary human family can embrace [...] The heart of the priest, in order that it may be available for this service, for this commitment of love, must be free. Celibacy is a sign of a

---

[362]    Cf. ECUMENICAL COUNCIL VATICAN II, Decree *Presbyterorum Ordinis*, 16; *C.I.C.*, cann. 1036; 1037.

[363]    Cf. *Pontificale Romanum, De ordinatione Episcopi, Presbyterorum et Diaconorum*, III, 228, *l.c.*, 134; JOHN PAUL II, *Letter to Priests for Holy Thursday 1979* (8 April 1979), 9: *l.c.*, 409-411.

[364]    Cf. SYNOD OF BISHOPS, Document on the Ministerial Priesthood *Ultimis temporibus* (30 November 1971), II, I, 4: *l.c.*, 916-917.

[365]    Cf. ECUMENICAL COUNCIL VATICAN II, Decree *Presbyterorum Ordinis*, 16.

[366]    Cf. *ibid.*

freedom that exists for the sake of service. According to this sign, the hierarchical or 'ministerial' priesthood is, according to the tradition of our Church, more strictly 'ordered' to the common priesthood of the faithful"[367].

## The Example of Jesus

81. Celibacy, therefore, is gift of self "in" and "with" Christ to his Church and expresses the service of the priest to the Church "in" and "with" the Lord[368].

The example is the Lord himself, who, going against what may be considered the dominant culture of his time, freely chose to live celibate. In following him the disciples left behind 'everything' in order to carry out the mission entrusted to them (*Lk* 18:28-30).

For this reason the Church, from apostolic times, has wished to conserve the gift of perpetual continence on the part of the clergy and chooses the candidates for Holy Orders from among the celibate faithful (Cf. *2Th* 2:15; *1Cor* 7:5; 9,5; *1Tm* 3:2.12; 5,9; *Tt* 1:6.8)[369].

---

[367] JOHN PAUL II, *Letter to Priests for Holy Thursday 1979* (8 April 1979), 8: *Insegnamenti* II/1 (1979), 841-862.

[368] Cf. JOHN PAUL II, Post-Synodal Apostolic Exhortation *Pastores dabo vobis*, 29.

[369] For the interpretation of these texts, cf. COUNCIL OF ELVIRA (a. 305), cann. 27; 33: BRUNS HERM., *Canones Apostolorum et Conciliorum saec. IV-VI* II, 5-6; COUNCIL OF NEOCESAREA (a. 314), can. 1: *Pont. Commissio ad redigendum CIC Orientalis*, IX, I/2, 74-82; ECUMENICAL COUNCIL OF NICAEA I (a. 325), can. 3: *Conc. Oecum. Decr.*, 6; COUNCIL OF CARTHAGE (a. 390): *Concilia Africae a. 345-525, CCL* 149, 13, 133ss; ROMAN SYNOD (a. 386): *Conc. Oecum. Decr.*, 58-63; COUNCIL OF TRULLANO II (a. 691), cann. 3, 6, 12, 13, 26, 30, 48: *Pont. Commissio ad redigendum CIC Orientalis*, IX, I/1, 125-186; SIRICIO, decretale *Directa* (a. 386): *PL* 13, 1131-1147; INNOCENT I, Letter *Dominus inter* (a. 405): BRUNS cit. 274-277; ST. LEO THE GREAT, Letter *a Rusticus* (a. 456): *PL* 54, 1191; EUSEBIUS OF CESAREA, *Demonstratio Evangelica*, 1, 9: *PG*, 22, 82; EPIPHANIO OF SALAMINA, *Panarion: PG* 41, 868. 1024; *Expositio Fidei, PG* 42, 823 ff.

Celibacy is a gift received from divine mercy[370] as the choice freely and gratefully accepting a particular vocation of love for God and others. It must not be understood and lived as if it were no more than a collateral effect of the priesthood.

## Difficulties and Objections

82. In today's cultural climate often conditioned by a vision of man lacking in values, and above all incapable of giving a full, positive and liberating sense to human sexuality, often posed is the question about the importance and meaning of priestly celibacy, or at least of how opportune it is to assert its close bond and profound harmony with the ministerial priesthood.

"In a certain sense, this continuous criticism against celibacy may surprise in a time when it is becoming increasingly fashionable not to get married. But this not-getting married is something totally, fundamentally different from celibacy. The avoidance of marriage is based on a will to live only for oneself, of not accepting any definitive tie, to have the life of every moment in full autonomy, to decide at any time what to do, what to take from life; and therefore a 'no' to the bond, a 'no' to definitiveness, to have life for oneself alone. While celibacy is just the opposite: it is a definitive 'yes'. It is to let oneself be taken in the hand of God, to give oneself into the hands of the Lord, into his 'I'. And therefore, it is an act of loyalty and trust, an act that also implies the fidelity of marriage. It is the opposite of this 'no', of this autonomy that accepts no obligations, which will not enter into a bond"[371].

The priest announces not himself, "but within and through his own humanity every priest must be well aware that he is bringing to the world another, God himself. God is the

[370] Cf. SACRED CONGREGATION FOR CATHOLIC EDUCATION, *Educative Orientations for Formation to Priestly Celibacy* (11 April 1974), 16: *l.c.*, 200-201.

[371] BENEDICT XVI, *Prayer Vigil on the Occasion of the Conclusion of the Year for Priests* (10 June 2010): *l.c.*, 397-406

only treasure which ultimately people desire to find in a priest"[372]. The priestly model is that of being a witness of the absolute; the fact that in many ambits celibacy is known or appreciated very little at present must not lead to speculation about different scenarios, but calls for the rediscovery in a new way of this gift of God's love for man. In fact, priestly celibacy is also admired and loved by many non-Christian persons.

It cannot be forgotten that celibacy is vivified by the practice of the virtue of chastity, which can be lived only through the cultivation of purity with supernatural and human maturity[373] insofar as essential for the development of the talent of the vocation. It is not possible to love Christ and others with an impure heart. The virtue of purity makes it possible to live what the Apostle said: "Therefore, glorify God in your body!" (*1Cor* 6:20). Then again, when this virtue is lacking, all the other dimensions are damaged. While it is true that today's world poses various difficulties regarding the living of holy purity, it is all the truer that the Lord abundantly showers his grace and offers the practical means for practicing this virtue with joy and happiness.

It is clear that in order to guarantee and protect this gift in a climate of serene equilibrium and spiritual progress, practiced must be all those measures that avert possible difficulties for priests[374].

---

[372] BENEDICT XVI, *Address to the Participants at the Plenary of the Congregation for the Clergy* (16 March 2009): *l.c.*, 393.

[373] Cf. JOHN PAUL II, Post-Synodal Apostolic Exhortation *Pastores dabo vobis*, 29; 50; CONGREGATION FOR CATHOLIC EDUCATION, Instruction *In continuità* on vocation discernment criteria regarding persons with homosexual tendencies in view of their admission to the Seminary and to Sacred Orders (4 November 2005): *AAS* 97 (2005), 1007-1013; *Educative Orientations for Formation to Priestly Celibacy* (11 April 1974): *EV* 5 (1974-1976), 188-256.

[374] Cf. ST. JOHN CHRYSOSTOM, *De Sacerdotio*, VI, 2: *PG* 48, 679: "The soul of the priest must be purer than the rays of the sun so that the Holy Spirit not abandon him and so that he might say: *It is no longer I that live but Christ that lives in me* (Gal. 2:20). If the anachorites of the desert who lived far from the city and its activity, enjoying harbour and the tranquility there, they neverthe-

It is therefore necessary for priests to conduct themselves with due prudence in their dealings with persons whose company could endanger fidelity to the gift or cause scandal among the faithful[375]. In particular cases priests must submit to the judgment of the Bishop, whose obligation it is to establish precise rules in this regard[376]. Quite logically, the priest must abstain from any ambiguous conduct and not forget his primary duty to bear witness to the redemptive love of Christ. In this area, unfortunately, some situations that have occurred have caused great damage to the Church and its credibility, even though there have been many more such situations in the world. The current context also demands on the part of priests an even greater sensitivity and prudence regarding relations with children and wards[377]. In particular, avoided must be situations that could give rise to rumours (for example, letting children enter the parish house on their own or accompanying minors in a car, etc.). Regarding confession, it would be opportune for children to go to confession in the confessional when the church is open to the public, or else, if for some reason it proved necessary to act otherwise, that the corresponding norms of prudence be respected.

Priests are not to fail from following those ascetical norms

less did not rely solely on the security of that life of theirs, but rather took special care of strengthening themselves in purity and confidence and diligently ensuring to the best of their ability that their conduct be worthy of God's presence. To what extent, do you think, must a priest employ strength and violence to avoid any kind of stain against his spiritual beauty? Certainly he needs to have more purity than monks. Yet precisely he who needs it the most is the one who most often is exposed to inevitable occasions in which he can be contaminated, unless he renders this inaccessible with assiduous sobriety and vigilance".

[375]    Cf. *C.I.C.*, can. 277, § 2.

[376]    Cf. *ibid.*, can. 277, § 3.

[377]    Cf. JOHN PAUL II, Litterae apostolicae Motu Proprio datae *Sacramentorum sanctitatis tutela quibus Normae de gravioribus delictis Congregationi pro Doctrina Fidei reservatis promulgantur* (30 April 2001): *AAS* 93 (2001), 737-739 (modified by Benedict XVI on 21 May 2010: *AAS* 102 (2010) 419-430).

proven by the experience of the Church and required even more so in present day circumstances. They are to prudently avoid frequenting places, attending shows, reading materials or surfing Internet sites that constitute a threat to the observance of celibate chastity[378] or an occasion or cause for grave sins against Christian morals. When making use of the means of social communication for pastoral purposes or leisure they are to observe the necessary discretion and avoid anything that could cause harm to their vocation.

To safeguard lovingly the gift received in today's climate of exasperated sexual permissiveness, priests are to use all the natural and supernatural means abounding in the tradition of the Church. On one hand, priestly friendship, sound relations with persons, asceticism and self control, mortification; it is also useful to encourage a culture of beauty in the various realms of life that could help with respect to everything that is degrading and harmful, nourish resolute passion for one's apostolic ministry, serenely accept solitude, and exercise a wise and worthwhile management of free time so it does not become empty time. Essential in the same sense are communion with Christ, an intense Eucharistic piety, frequent confession, spiritual direction, retreats and days of recollection, a spirit of acceptance of crosses in daily life, trust and love for the Church, filial devotion to the Blessed Virgin Mary, and consideration of the examples of holy priests of all times[379].

Difficulties and objections have always accompanied the Latin Church and some Oriental Churches down through the centuries in conferring the priestly ministry only upon those men who have received the gift of chastity in celibacy from God. The discipline of the other Oriental Churches that do admit the married priesthood is not in opposition with that of the Latin Church. In fact, these Oriental Churches nonetheless

---

[378]  Cf. ECUMENICAL COUNCIL VATICAN II, Decree *Presbyterorum Ordinis*, 16.

[379]  Cf. PAUL VI, Encyclical Letter *Sacerdotalis caelibatus*, 79-81; JOHN PAUL II, Post-Synodal Apostolic Exhortation *Pastores dabo vobis*, 29.

require celibacy of Bishops. Moreover, they do not permit the matrimony of priests and do not allow priest widowers to re-marry. It is always and only a matter of the Ordination of men already married.

The objections still being raised by some people today against priestly celibacy are often based on specious arguments, such as, for example, accusations that it reflects a disincarnated spiritualism or entails suspicion or scorn towards sexuality; other accusations are based on the consideration of sad and sorrowful cases, which are always particular ones, which people tend to generalise. Forgotten, however, is the witness offered by the overwhelming majority of priests, who live their celibacy with interior liberty, rich evangelical motivations and spiritual fecundity in a horizon of convinced and joyful fidelity to their vocation and mission, without even mentioning the many laypersons who happily take upon themselves fecund apostolic celibacy.

## 2.11. The Priestly Spirit of Poverty

*Poverty as Availability*

83. The poverty of Jesus has a salvific scope. Christ, being rich, became poor for us so that by his poverty we might become rich. (cf. *2Cor* 8:9).

The Letter to the Philippians reveals the relationship between the giving of self and the spirit of service that must animate the pastoral ministry. In fact, St. Paul says Jesus did not consider "his equality to God something to cling to, but empties himself to assume the condition of a slave" (*Ph* 2:6-7). In all truth, it will be difficult for a priest to become a true servant and minister of his brothers if he is concerned about his own comforts and well being.

Through his condition as a poor man Christ manifests that he has received everything from eternity from the Father and returns everything to him unto the complete offering of His life.

The example of Christ poor must lead the priest to conform himself to Him, with interior detachment regarding all the world's goods and riches[380]. The Lord teaches us that the true good is God and that true richness is attaining eternal life: "For what does it profit a man if he gains the whole world, but suffers the loss of his soul? Or what will a man give in exchange for his soul?" (*Mk* 8:36-37). Each priest is called to live the virtue of poverty which consists essentially in consigning his heart to Christ as the true treasure, and not to material things.

The priest, whose inheritance is the Lord (cf. *Nb* 18:20)[381], knows that his mission, like that of the Church, takes place in the midst of the world and that created goods are necessary for the personal development of man. Nonetheless, he will use such goods with a sense of responsibility, moderation, upright intention and detachment proper to him who has his treasure in heaven and knows that everything is to be used for the edification of the Kingdom of God (*Lk* 10:7; *Mt* 10:9-10; *1Cor* 9:14; *Ga* 6:6)[382]. He will therefore abstain from those lucrative activities that are not consonant with his ministry[383]. Moreover, the priest must avoid offering grounds for even the slightest insinuation that he may conceive his ministry also as an opportunity for obtaining benefits, favouring friends and relatives or seeking positions of privilege. Quite on the contrary, he must be in the midst of all in order to serve others unreservedly, following the example of Christ, the Good Shepherd (cf. *Jn* 10:10). Moreover, recalling that the gift he has received is gratuitous, he is to be disposed to give in like manner (*Mt* 10:8;

---

[380] Cf. ECUMENICAL COUNCIL VATICAN II, Decree *Presbyterorum Ordinis*, 17; 20-21.

[381] Cf. BENEDICT XVI, *Address to the Roman Curia* (22 December 2006): *AAS*, 98 (2006).

[382] Cf. ECUMENICAL COUNCIL VATICAN II, Decree *Presbyterorum Ordinis*, 17; JOHN PAUL II, *General Audience* (21 July 1993), 3: *Insegnamenti* XVI/2 (1993), 89-90.

[383] Cf. *C.I.C.*, cann. 286; 1392.

*Ac* 8:18-25)[384] and use what he receives for the exercise of his office for the good of the Church and works of charity, after having provided for his honest sustenance and the fulfilment of all the duties of his state[385].

Lastly, even though the priest does not make a public promise of poverty, it is incumbent upon him to lead a simple life and abstain from whatever may smack of worldliness[386], thereby embracing voluntary poverty in order to follow Christ more closely[387]. In all aspects (living quarters, means of transportation, vacations, etc.) the priest is to eliminate any kind of affectation and luxury[388]. In this sense the priest must battle every day in order not to lapse into consumerism and the easy life that pervade society in many parts of the world. A serious examination of conscience will help him to assess his tenor of life, his readiness to attend to the faithful and perform his duties; to ask himself if the means and things he uses respond to true need or if he may not be seeking convenience and comfort, taking flight from sacrifice. Precisely at stake in the consistency between what he says and what he does, especially with respect to poverty, are the priest's credibility and apostolic effectiveness.

Friend of the poorest, he will reserve his most refined and delicate pastoral charity for them, with a preferential option for all the old and new poverties so tragically present in the world, ever recalling that the first misery from which man must be liberated is sin, the ultimate root of all evil.

---

[384] Cf. ECUMENICAL COUNCIL VATICAN II, Decree *Presbyterorum Ordinis*, 17.

[385] Cf. *ibid.*; *C.I.C.*, cann. 282; 222, § 2; 529, § 1.

[386] Cf. *C.I.C.*, can. 282, § 1.

[387] Cf. ECUMENICAL COUNCIL VATICAN II, Decree *Presbyterorum Ordinis*, 17.

[388] Cf. *ibid.*, 17.

## 2.12. Devotion to Mary

*Imitating the Virtues of our Mother*

84. There is an "essential relationship between the Mother of Jesus and the priesthood of the ministers of the Son" issuing forth from the one existing between the divine motherhood of Mary and the priesthood of Christ[389].

Rooted in this relationship is the Marian spirituality of each priest. The priestly spirituality may not be considered complete if it does not take into serious consideration the testament of Christ crucified, when he willed to entrust his Mother to the beloved disciple, and through him to all the priests called to continues his work of redemption.

Just like to John at the foot of the Cross, entrusted to each priest in a special way is Mary as Mother (cf. *Jn* 19:26-27).

Priests are among the disciples most loved by the crucified and risen Jesus and they are to welcome Mary as their Mother in their own life, making her the object of constant attention and prayer. The ever Virgin Mary therefore becomes the Mother who leads them to Christ, makes them sincerely love the Church, intercedes for them, and guides them towards the Kingdom of heaven.

85. Every priest knows that Mary, because she is Mother, is also the most eminent formator of his priesthood, since it is she who knows how to model his priestly heart, protect him from dangers, fatigue and discouragement, and, with maternal solicitude, watch over him so he may grow in wisdom and grace before God and men (cf. *Lk* 2:40).

But priests are not devout sins if they know not how to imitate their Mother's virtues. Every priest will therefore look to Mary in order to be a humble, obedient and chaste minister,

[389] Cf. JOHN PAUL II, *General Audience* (30 June 1993): *Insegnamenti* XVI/1 (1993), 1689-1699.

and the bear witness to charity in total oblation to the Lord and the Church[390].

## The Eucharist and Mary

86. In each Eucharist celebration we hear anew those words "Woman, here is your son" said by the Son to his Mother, while He himself repeats to us: "This is your Mother!" (*Jn* 19:26-27). Living the Eucharist also implies ceaselessly receiving this gift: "Mary is a *'woman of the Eucharist'* in her whole *life*. The Church, which looks to Mary as a model, is also called to imitate her in her relationship with this most holy mystery. [...] Mary is present, with the Church and as the Mother of the Church, at each of our celebrations of the Eucharist. If the Church and the Eucharist are inseparably united, the same ought to be said of Mary and the Eucharist"[391]. In this way the encounter with Jesus in the Sacrifice of the Altar inevitably entails the encounter with Mary, his Mother. In fact, "through his identification and sacramental conformation to Jesus, Son of God and Son of Mary, every priest can and must truly feel himself the beloved son of this most high and most humble Mother"[392].

Masterpiece of the priestly sacrifice of Christ, the ever Virgin Mother of God represents the Church in the purest way, "with neither stain nor wrinkle", completely "holy and immaculate" (*Eph* 5:27). This contemplation of the Blessed Virgin – along whose side is St. Joseph, the master of interior life – places before the priest the ideal to pursue in the ministry of his community so this community as well may be "glorious" (*ibid.*) through the priestly gift of his own life.

---

[390] Cf. ECUMENICAL COUNCIL VATICAN II, Decree *Presbyterorum Ordinis*, 18.

[391] JOHN PAUL II, Encyclical Letter *Ecclesia de Eucharistia* (17 April 2003): *l.c.*, 53; 57.

[392] BENEDICT XVI, *General Audience* (12 August 2009): *Insegnamenti* V/2 (2009), 94.

# III. ONGOING FORMATION

The priest has a constant need to deepen his formation. Even if on the day of his ordination he received the permanent seal that configured him *in æternum* with Christ Head and Shepherd, he is called to ongoing development in order to be more effective in his ministry. In this sense it is fundamental for priests to be aware that their formation did not come to an end during the years in the seminary. On the contrary, as of the very day of his ordination the priest must feel the need to make constant progress in order to be ever more of Christ the Lord.

## 3.1. Principles

*The Need for Ongoing Formation Today*

87. As Benedict XVI has recalled: "The theme of the priestly identity [...] is determinant for the exercise of the ministerial priesthood in the present and in the future"[393]. These words of the Holy Father constitute the point of reference upon which to base the ongoing formation of the clergy: help them to deepen what it means to be a priest. "The priest's fundamental relationship is to Jesus Christ, Head and Shepherd"[394], and in this sense ongoing formation should be a means to heighten this "exclusive" relationship that necessarily has an impact on everything a priest is and does. Ongoing formation is a requirement that begins and develops from the moment of receiving the Sacrament of Holy Orders, with which the priest is not only "consecrated" by the Father, "sent" by the Son, but also "animated" by the Holy Spirit. This

---

[393] BENEDICT XVI, *Address to the Participants at the Theological Conference Organised by the Congregation for the Clergy* (12 March 2010): l.c., 323-326.

[394] JOHN PAUL II, Post-Synodal Apostolic Exhortation *Pastores dabo vobis*, 16.

formation is destined to involve and progressively assimilate the entire life and activity of the priest in fidelity to the gift received: "That is why I am reminding you now to fan into a flame the gift that God gave you when I laid my hands on you" (*2Tm* 1:6).

This necessity is intrinsic to the divine gift itself[395] which is to be continually 'vivified' so the priest may adequately respond to his vocation. In fact, as a man situated in history, he needs to perfect himself in all the aspects of his human and spiritual existence in order to attain that conformity with Christ, the unifying principle of all things.

Rapid and widespread transformations and the often secularised tissue of society so typical of the world in which we live are likewise factors that render absolutely unavoidable each priest's duty to be suitably prepared in order not to attenuate his identity and to respond to the needs of the new evangelisation. Corresponding to this serious duty is a precise right on the part of the faithful, who positively feel the effects of the good formation and holiness of their priests[396].

88. The spiritual life of the priest and his pastoral ministry go hand in hand with the ongoing work on them – correspondence to the Holy Spirit's work of sanctification – that makes it possible to deepen and bring together in a harmonious manner the diverse spheres of formation: spiritual, human, intellectual and pastoral. This work must begin in the seminary and must be supported by the Bishops at the various levels: national, regional, and above all diocesan.

It is encouraging to note that there are already many Ecclesiastic Circumscriptions and Episcopal Conferences actively involved in promising endeavours for an authentic ongoing formation of their priests. It is hoped that all Dioceses may be able to respond to this need. Where this may not be possible at present, however, it is advisable for them to work out agreements among themselves or establish contacts with those insti-

---

[395]  Cf. *ibid.*, 70.
[396]  Cf. *ibid.*

tutions or persons particularly well prepared to perform such a delicate task[397].

## Instrument of Sanctification

89. Ongoing formation is a means necessary for the priest to attain the aim of his vocation, that being the service of God and his people.

In practical terms it consists in helping all priests to respond generously to the commitment required by the dignity and responsibility God has conferred upon them by the Sacrament of Holy Orders; in safeguarding, defending and developing their specific identity and vocation; in sanctifying themselves and others through the exercise of the sacred ministry.

This means that priests must avoid any dualism between spirituality and ministry, the profound origin of some crises.

It is evident that in order to achieve this aim of a supernatural order, discovered must be the general criteria on which the ongoing formation of priests must be structured and organised.

Such general criteria or principles of organisation must be conceived on the basis of the aim proposed, or, all the better, sought in that aim.

## It Must be Imparted by the Church

90. Ongoing formation is a right-duty of the priest and imparting it is a right-duty of the Church. It is therefore stipulated in universal law[398]. In fact, in the same way the vocation to the sacred ministry is received in the Church, only upon the Church is it incumbent to impart the specific formation in keeping with the responsibility proper to that ministry. Therefore, ongoing formation, insofar as an activity linked to the exercise of the ministerial priesthood, pertains to the responsibility of the Pope and the Bishops. Hence, it is the duty and the

---

[397]    Cf. *ibid.*, 79.
[398]    Cf. *C.I.C.*, can. 279.

right of the Church to continue forming its ministers, helping them to progress in their generous response to the gift God has bestowed on them.

On his part, and as a requirement of the gift granted with Ordination, the priest has also received the right to receive the necessary help from the Church in order to carry out his service effectively and in a holy manner.

## It must be Ongoing

91. Formation as an activity is based on a dynamic demand intrinsic to the ministerial charism, which in itself is permanent and irreversible. Therefore, neither the Church that imparts it nor the minister who receives it may ever consider it over and done. It is therefore necessary that it be thought out and developed in such a way that *all* priests may receive it *always,* keeping ever in mind characteristics and possibilities that vary with age, condition of life and assignments[399].

## It Must be Complete

92. Such formation must encompass and harmonise all the dimensions of priestly formation; that is to say it must tend to assist each priest: to attain the development of a human personality matured in the spirit of service to others in whatever task assigned to him; to be intellectually prepared in the theological sciences in harmony with the *Magisterium* of the Church[400], as well as in the human sciences insofar as related with his ministry, in order to carry out with greater effective-

---

[399]   Cf. JOHN PAUL II, Post-Synodal Apostolic Exhortation *Pastores dabo vobis,* 76.

[400]   Cf.   CONGREGATION FOR THE   DOCTRINE OF THE   FAITH, Instruction *Donum veritatis* on the Ecclesial Vocation of the Theologian (24 May 1990), 21-41: *AAS* 82 (1990), 1559-1569; INTERNATIONAL THEOLOGICAL COMMISSION, *Theses Rationes magisterii cum theologia* on the Mutual Relationship between the *Magisterium* of the Church and Theology (6 June 1976), thesis n. 8: "Gregorianum" 57 (1976), 549-556.

ness his role as a witness of the faith; to have a solid spiritual life nourished by intimacy with Jesus Christ and love for the Church; and to carry out his pastoral ministry with commitment and dedication.

In practice, such formation must be complete: human, spiritual, intellectual, pastoral, systematic and personalised.

*Human Formation*

93. Human formation is particularly important since "the whole work of priestly formation would be deprived of its necessary foundation if it lacked a suitable human formation[401]; objectively speaking it constitutes the platform and foundation on which it is possible to construct the edifice of intellectual, spiritual and pastoral formation. The priest must not forget that, "chosen from among men, [...] he remains one of them and is called to serve them by giving his life to God"[402]. Therefore, as a brother among brothers, in order to sanctify himself and succeed in his priestly mission he is to have the resources of human virtues that make him worthy of the respect of others. It must be recalled that "it is important for the priest, who is called to accompany others through the journey of life up to the threshold of death, to have the right balance of heart and mind, reason and feeling, body and soul, and to be humanly integrated"[403].

In particular, with his gaze ever on Christ, the priest is to practice goodness of heart, patience, kindness, strength of soul, love for justice, even-mindedness, fidelity to his word, and coherence with the commitments freely assumed, etc.[404]. In this field, ongoing formation fosters growth in the human virtues,

---

[401]    JOHN PAUL II, Post-Synodal Apostolic Exhortation *Pastores dabo vobis*, 43; cf. ECUMENICAL COUNCIL VATICAN II, Decree *Optatam totius*, 11.

[402]    BENEDICT XVI, *Video Message to the Participants at the International Priests' Retreat* (27 September-3 October 2009): *Insegnamenti* V/2 (2009), 300-303.

[403]    BENEDICT XVI, *Letter to Seminarians* (18 October 2010), 6: *l.c.*, 797-798.

[404]    Cf. ECUMENICAL COUNCIL VATICAN II, Decree *Presbyterorum Ordinis*, 3.

helping priests to always live "unity of life in the exercise of the ministry"[405], from cordiality in demeanour to the ordinary rules of good conduct or the ability to be present in any context.

There is a connection between human life and spiritual life that depends on the unity of soul and body proper to human nature, and this is why where grave human deficits remain, the "structure" of the personality is never safe from sudden "collapses".

It is likewise important for the priest to reflect on his social conduct, correctness and good manners – which are also born of charity and humility – in the various forms of human relations, as well as on the values of friendship and gentleman-like ways, etc.

Lastly, in today's cultural situation this formation must be designed to contribute – with recourse if necessary to the assistance of the psychological sciences[406] – to human maturation: albeit difficult to specify in contents, this undoubtedly implies equilibrium and harmony in the integration of propensities and values, psychological and affective stability, prudence, objectivity in judgment, fortitude in self-control, sociability, etc. In this way priests, especially young ones, are helped to live chastity, modesty and prudence with due tact, particularly in the prudent use of television and Internet.

Indeed, especially important is formation in the use of Internet, and in the use of the new technologies of communication in general. Moderation and temperance are necessary in order to avoid obstacles in the way of the life of intimacy with God. The "web world" offers considerable potentialities with a view to evangelisation, and yet when ill handled or managed they can also cause grave damage to souls; at times, under the pretext of a better use of time or the need to be informed, it is

---

[405] *Ibid.*, 14.

[406] Cf. CONGREGATION FOR CATHOLIC EDUCATION, *Ogni vocazione* Orientations for the use of Psychological Competencies in the Admission and Formation of Candidates to the Priesthood (29 June 2008), 5: "L'Osservatore Romano", 31 October 2008, 4s.

possible to foment a form of disordered curiosity that hampers the ever necessary recollection from which the efficacy of the commitment issues forth.

In this same line of thought, even if the use of Internet constitutes an useful opportunity to bring the announcement of the Gospel to many persons, the priest is to exercise prudence and reflection in assessing his involvement in order not to take time away from his pastoral ministry as regards the preaching of the Word of God, the celebration of the sacraments, spiritual direction, etc., where his presence cannot be replaced. In any case, his participation in these new ambits is always to reflect special charity, supernatural sense, moderation and temperance so that one and all will feel attracted not by the figure of the priest, but rather by the Person of our Lord Jesus Christ.

### Spiritual Formation

94. Keeping in mind what has already been presented in detail, the following considerations will deal with some practical means of formation.

It would be necessary above all to deepen understanding of the principal aspects of priestly existence by referring in particular to biblical, patristic, theological and hagiographic teachings in which the priest must be constantly updated not only by reading good books, but also by attending study courses, conferences, etc.[407].

Specific sessions could also be devoted to care in the celebration of the sacraments, as well as to questions of spirituality such as the Christian and human virtues, the way of praying, and the relationship between the spiritual life and the liturgical and pastoral ministry, etc.

More specifically, it is hoped that each priest, perhaps dur-

---

[407] Cf. ECUMENICAL COUNCIL VATICAN II, Decree *Presbyterorum Ordinis*, 19; Decree *Optatam totius*, 22; *C.I.C.*, can. 279, § 2; SACRED CONGREGATION FOR CATHOLIC EDUCATION, *Ratio Fundamentalis Institutionis Sacerdotalis* (19 March 1985), 101.

ing periodical retreats, would draw up a concrete plan of personal life in concord with his spiritual director. The following elements may be suggested: 1. daily meditation on the Word or a mystery of the faith; 2. daily personal encounter with Jesus in the Eucharist, in addition to devote celebration of Mass and frequent confession; 3. Marian devotion (Rosary, consecration or entrustment, intimate colloquy); 4. a period of doctrinal formation and study of the history of the saints; 5. due rest; 6. renewed commitment in putting into practice the indications of one's Bishop and verification of one's convinced adhesion to the *Magisterium* and to ecclesiastical discipline; 7. attention to priestly communion, friendship and fraternity. Likewise to be deepened are other aspects such as the administration of one's time and goods, work, and the importance of working with others.

## *Intellectual Formation*

95. Considering the enormous influence that humanistic-philosophical schools of thought have on modern culture, as well as the fact that priests have not always received adequate preparation in such disciplines, also because they come from different educational backgrounds, during encounters it is necessary to keep in mind the humanistic and philosophical themes of greatest relevance, or which in any case "have a relationship with the sacred sciences, particularly insofar as they may be useful in the exercise of the pastoral ministry"[408].

Such themes also constitute a valid form of support for dealing correctly with the principal arguments of Sacred Scripture, fundamental, dogmatic and moral theology, liturgy, Canon Law, ecumenism, etc., recalling that the teaching of these subjects must not excessively develop the insurgence of problems or remain in the realms of theory or mere information, but lead to genuine formation, which is prayer, communion and pastoral enterprise. Moreover, dedicating time – possi-

---

[408] *C.I.C.*, can. 279, § 3; CONGREGATION FOR CATHOLIC EDUCATION, Decree *Reforming Ecclesiastical Studies in Philosophy* (28 gennaio 2011), 8 ff: *AAS* 103 (2011), 148 ff.

bly each day – to the study of manuals or essays of philosophy, theology and Canon Law will be of great assistance for deepening the *sentire cum Ecclesia*; in this task the *Catechism of the Catholic Church* and its *Compendium* constitute a most valuable reference instrument.

It should be seen to it that during priestly encounters the documents of the *Magisterium* are deepened in a community manner and under authoritative guidance, so that facilitated in the diocesan apostolate would be that unity of interpretation and praxis so beneficial to the work of evangelisation.

Particular importance in intellectual formation is to be given to the studying of themes and issues that are of greater relevance today in cultural debate and in pastoral praxis, such as, for example, themes dealing with social ethics, bioethics, etc.

Special treatment must be reserved to the questions posed by scientific progress, which exercises such an influence on the way people think and live. The priest is not to dispense himself from keeping adequately updated and ready to give the reason for his hope (cf. *1Pt* 3:15) in the face of the questions the faithful – many of whom have a elevated cultural level – may pose, since they are cognisant of the progress made by the sciences. In this regard the priest will not fail to consult due experts and sure doctrine. Indeed, when presenting the Word of God the priest must take into consideration the progressive growth of the intellectual formation of people, and hence be able to adapt according to their level, as well as to various groups and their places of origin.

It is of utmost interest to study, deepen and diffuse the social doctrine of the Church. Following the thrust of magisterial teachings, it is necessary for attention to the needy on the part of all priests, and through them all the faithful, not remain on the level of pious wishes, but become a concrete commitment in life. "Today more than ever, the Church is aware that her social message will gain credibility more immediately from the *witness of actions* than as a result of its logic and internal consistency"[409].

---

[409] Cf. JOHN PAUL II, Encyclical Letter *Centesimus annus* (1 May 1991), 57: *AAS* 83 (1991), 862-863.

An indispensable requirement for the intellectual formation of priests is familiarity with and prudent use of the *means of
social communication* in their ministerial activities. When well
used, these means constitute a providential instrument of
evangelisation, since they are able not only to reach great
masses of the faithful at a distance, but also have an profound
impact on their minds and their behaviour.

In this regard it would be opportune for the Bishop or the
Episcopal Conference itself to prepare programs and technical
instruments suited to that end. Likewise, the priest must avoid
being protagonist prone so that standing out in the limelight
before men and women is not his person, but our Lord Jesus.

*Pastoral Formation*

96. For adequate pastoral formation it is necessary to hold
encounters whose main objective is reflection of the pastoral
plan of the Diocese. Not lacking in said encounters should also
be treatment of all issues and questions related to the life and
pastoral work of the priests; for example, fundamental morals,
the ethics of professional and social life, etc. Particularly inter-
esting may be the organisation of courses or seminars on the
apostolate of the Sacrament of Confession[410] or on practical
questions of spiritual direction in both general and specific
situations. Practical formation in the field of the liturgy is also
particularly important. Special attention should be reserved to
learning how to celebrate the Mass well – as pointed out ear-
lier, the *ars celebrandi* is a *sine qua non* condition of the *actuosa
partecipatio* of the faithful – and to adoration outside the Mass.

Other themes that could most usefully dealt with may be:
catechesis, the family, priestly and religious vocations, knowledge of the life and spirituality of the saints, youth, the elderly,

---

[410]   Cf. PONTIFICAL COUNCIL FOR THE FAMILY, *Cristo continua,*
Document namely a "Vademecum" for Confessors on Certain Moral Themes
Pertaining to Conjugal Life (12 February 1997): "L'Osservatore Romano", 2
March 1997, tabloid insert.

the infirm, ecumenism, the so-called 'lapsed' brethren, bio-ethical issues, etc.

Considering circumstances at present it is very important for the pastoral plan to include the organisation of special cycles of courses to deepen and assimilate the *Catechism of the Catholic Church,* which, especially for priests, constitutes a valuable instrument for preaching and for the work of evangelisation in general.

## It Must be Organic and Complete

97. In order for ongoing formation to be complete it is necessary for it to be structured "not as something haphazard, but as a systematic offering of subjects, which unfolds by stages and takes on precise forms"[411]. This involves the need to create a certain organisational structure that establishes in an opportune manner instruments, times and subjects for its concrete and adequate implementation. In this sense there will be useful feedback into the life of the priest on themes such as: the knowledge of the Scriptures in their entirety, the Fathers of the Church and the great Councils; each of the contents of the faith in its unity; essential matters of moral theology and the social doctrine of the Church; ecumenical theology and fundamental orientation regarding the great religions with respect to ecumenical, inter-religious and inter-cultural dialogue; philosophy and Canon Law[412].

Such organisation must be accompanied by habitual personal study, since even periodical studies would be of little use if not accompanied by personal application to study[413].

[411]    JOHN PAUL II, Post-Synodal Apostolic Exhortation *Pastores dabo vobis,* 79.

[412]    Cf. SACRED CONGREGATION FOR CATHOLIC EDUCATION, *Ratio fundamentalis institutionis sacerdotalis,* 76ff.

[413]    Cf. JOHN PAUL II, Post-Synodal Apostolic Exhortation *Pastores dabo vobis,* 79.

*It Must be Personalised*

98. Although imparted to all, the direct objective of ongoing formation is the service to each one of those receiving it. Therefore, together with collective or common means of formation, there must also be all those other means that tend to personalise the formation of each person.

Fostered for this reason, especially among those responsible for this service, is the awareness of having to reach each priest personally, attending to each one of them and not being satisfied with making the diverse opportunities available to them.

In his turn, each priest must feel he is encouraged, with the word and with the example of his Bishop and his confreres in the priesthood, to assume responsibility for his own formation, since he is the first formator of himself[414].

## 3.2. Organisation and Means

*Priestly Encounters*

99. The itinerary of priestly encounters must have a unitary character and proceed by stages.

Such unity must converge in conformation to Christ in such a way that the truth of faith, the spiritual life and the ministerial activity may lead to the progressive maturation of the entire presbytery.

The unified path of formation is paced by well defined stages. This will demand specific attention to the diverse age groupings of the priests, without overlooking any of them, as well as an assessment of the stages completed, with due care in synchronising common formation itineraries with personal ones, without which the former could have no effect.

The encounters of priests are to be considered necessary for growth in communion, ever increasing awareness and an adequate examination of the problems proper to each age group.

---

[414]   Cf. *ibid.*

Regarding the contents of such encounters, reference can be made to any themes proposed by the national and regional Episcopal Conferences. In any case, it is necessary for them to be established in a precise plan of formation of the Diocese, possibly updated each year[415].

Their organisation and actual holding may be prudently entrusted by the Bishop to faculties or institutes of theological and pastoral studies, seminaries, bodies or federations active in priestly formation[416], or any other specialised centre or institute, which, as possibilities and opportunities may counsel, may be diocesan, regional or national, as long as it has been ascertained that it does respond to the requirements of doctrinal orthodoxy, fidelity to the *Magisterium* and to ecclesiastical discipline, and does possess scientific expertise and adequate knowledge or real pastoral situations.

## *The Pastoral Year*

100. It will be the task of the Bishop, also through prudently selected forms of possible cooperation, to see to it that programmed for the year following ordination to the priesthood or the diaconate is the so-called pastoral year to ease the passage from the indispensable life in the seminary to the exercise of the sacred ministry, proceeding gradually and facilitating progressive and harmonious human and specifically priestly maturation[417].

During this year it will be necessary to ensure that the newly ordained priests are not immersed in excessively burden-

---

[415]   Cf. *ibid.*

[416]   Cf. *ibid.*; ECUMENICAL COUNCIL VATICAN II, Decree *Optatam totius*, 22; Decree *Presbyterorum Ordinis*, 19.

[417]   Cf. PAUL VI, Apostolic Letter *Ecclesiae Sanctae* (6 August 1966), I, 7: *AAS* 58 (1966), 761; SACRED CONGREGATION FOR THE CLERGY, Circular Letter to the Presidents of the Episcopal Conferences *Inter ea* (4 November 1969), 16: *l.c.*, 130-131; SACRED CONGREGATION FOR CATHOLIC EDUCATION, *Ratio Fundamentalis Institutionis Sacerdotalis*, 63; 101; *C.I.C.*, can. 1032, § 2.

some or delicate situations, and that they are not assigned to destinations where they would be working far away from their confreres. In fact, it will be good to foster some opportune form of common life insofar as possible.

This period of formation could be spent in a residence established for the purpose (House of the Clergy) or in a place that may constitute a precise and serene point of reference for all the priests dealing with their initial pastoral experiences. This will facilitate colloquy and discussion with the Bishop and one's confreres, prayer in common, in particular the Liturgy of the Hours, as well as the exercise of other fruitful practices of piety, such as adoration of the Blessed Sacrament, the holy Rosary, etc., the exchange of experiences, mutual encouragement, the flourishing of sound friendships.

It is opportune for the Bishop to direct newly ordained priests to confreres of exemplary life and pastoral zeal. Notwithstanding the often critical pastoral needs, the first destination should respond above all to the need to set young priests on the right path. The sacrifice of a year could then bear abundant fruits for the future.

It is not superfluous to underline the fact that this year, both delicate and precious, is to foster the full maturation of knowledge between the priest and his Bishop which began in the seminary and must become a true son-to-father relationship.

Regarding the intellectual part, this year is not to be that much of a period for learning new subjects, but rather for the in-depth assimilation and interiorisation of what was studied in institutional courses, in order to foster the formation of a mentality able to weigh details in the light of the plan of God[418].

In such a context there could be properly organized lessons and seminars regarding the practice of hearing of confessions, liturgy, catechesis, preaching, Canon Law, priestly, secu-

---

[418]   Cf. CONGREGATION FOR CATHOLIC EDUCATION, *Ratio Fundamentalis Institutionis Sacerdotalis*, 63.

lar and religious spirituality, social doctrine, communication and its means, knowledge of sects and new religions, etc.

In practice, the effort of synthesis must constitute the pathway along which this pastoral year proceeds. Each element must correspond to the fundamental project of the maturation of the spiritual life.

The successful outcome of the pastoral year is in any case and always conditioned by the personal commitment of the priest in question, who must each day strive for holiness in the continuous search for the means of sanctification that have helped him ever since his seminary days. Moreover, when there are practical difficulties in a diocese – shortage of priests, considerable pastoral work, etc. – regarding the organisation of a year with the aforementioned features, the Bishop must study how to adapt the diverse proposals for the pastoral year to the concrete situation, taking into account that it is of great importance for the formation and perseverance of young priests in the ministry.

## Times of Rest

101. The danger of routine, physical exhaustion due to the overwork to which priest are exposed especially today because of their ministry, and psychological fatigue caused by often having to battle against incomprehension, misunderstandings, prejudices, and going against organised and powerful forces that work to endorse in public the opinion whereby priests today belong to a culturally obsolete minority are likewise factors that can cause malaise in the soul of a pastor.

Notwithstanding urgent pastoral requirements, and precisely in order to be able to cope with them in an adequate manner, it is fitting for us to acknowledge our limits, and "find and have the humility, the courage to rest"[419]. Even though ordinary rest will normally be the most efficient means for regaining one's forces and continuing to work for the Kingdom

---

[419]    BENEDICT XVI, *Prayer Vigil on the Occasion of the Conclusion of the Year for Priests* (10 June 2010): *l.c.*, 397-406.

of God, it may be useful for priests to be granted more or less longer periods of time to spend with the Lord Jesus in a serene and intense manner, regaining the force and courage to forge ahead along the way to sanctification.

In order to respond to this particular requirement, already experimented in many places have been diverse initiatives, often with promising results. These experiences are valid and may be taken into consideration, despite the difficulties that may be encountered in some areas where the shortage of priests is more acutely felt.

For this purpose, monasteries, sanctuaries or other places of spirituality possibly located outside urban centres can play a considerable role, leaving the priest free from direct pastoral responsibilities for the period when he withdraws.

In some cases it may be useful to employ this time for purposes of study or updating in the sacred sciences, without forgetting the primary goal of renewing spiritual and apostolic vigour.

Accurately to be avoided in any case is the danger of considering these periods as mere vacation time or claiming them as a right; and all the more so should the priest feel the need on days of rest to celebrate the Eucharistic Sacrifice , the centre and origin of his life.

*The House of the Clergy*

102. Desirable wherever possible is the erection of a "House of the Clergy" where held could be the aforementioned formation counters, and which could also serve as premises for numerous other circumstances. This house should offer all those facilities and structures that may make it comfortable and attractive.

Wherever such a centre does not exist as of yet, and requirements may so suggest, it would be advisable to create structures on the national or regional level suited for the physical, psychological and spiritual recovery of priests.

*Days of Recollection and Retreats*

103. As the lengthy spiritual experience of the Church

demonstrates, days of recollection and retreats are suitable and efficacious instruments for an adequate ongoing formation of the clergy. Today as well do they remain necessary and timely. Against a practice that tends to empty man of everything that smacks of interiority, the priest must find God and himself by taking spiritual breaks in order to immerse himself in meditation and prayer.

For this reason Canon law stipulates that clerics "are obliged to make spiritual retreats, in accordance with the provision of particular law"[420]. The two most usual modes which may be prescribed by the Bishop in his own diocese are the day of recollection, possibly each month, and the annual retreat, lasting, for example, six days.

It is most fitting for the Bishop to plan and organise periodical days of recollection and annual retreats in such a way that each priest would be able to choose among those normally held, both inside and outside the diocese, by exemplary priests, priestly associations[421] or religious institutes especially experienced by virtue of their selfsame charism in spiritual formation, or monasteries.

Likewise advisable is the organisation of a special day of recollection for priests of recent ordination and in which the Bishop would actively participate[422].

It is important during such encounters to focus on spiritual themes, offer lengthy periods of silence and prayer, and attend with special care to the liturgical celebrations, the sacrament of penance, adoration of the Blessed Sacrament, spiritual direction, and acts of veneration and cult to the Blessed Virgin Mary.

In order to confer greater importance and efficacy upon these instruments of formation the Bishop could duly appoint

---

[420]    *C.I.C.*, can. 276, § 2, 4°; cf. cann. 533, § 2; 550, § 3.

[421]    Cf. ECUMENICAL COUNCIL VATICAN II, Decree *Presbyterorum Ordinis*, 8.

[422]    Cf. SACRED CONGREGATION FOR CATHOLIC EDUCATION, *Ratio Fundamentalis Institutionis Sacerdotalis*, 101.

a priest whose task would be to organise the times and ways of conducting them.

In any case, it is necessary for days of recollection and especially annual retreats to be lived as times of prayer and not as updating courses in theology and pastoral work.

### The Need for Programming

104. While acknowledging the customary difficulties of true ongoing formation especially due to the multiple and burdensome tasks to which priests are called, all difficulties may be surmounted if true and responsible commitment exists.

In keeping with the level of circumstances and to cope with the demands of the urgent work of evangelisation, also necessary is courageous pastoral action finalised to taking care of priests. By virtue of the force of charity, it is indispensable for the Bishop to demand that priests be generous in abiding by the legitimate dispositions made in this matter.

The existence of an "ongoing formation plan" means it must not only conceived or planned, but also implemented. Necessary to this end is a clear organisation of work, with *objectives, contents and instruments* to carry it out. "This responsibility leads the bishop, in communion with the presbyterate, to outline a project and establish a program which can ensure that ongoing formation is not something haphazard but a systematic offering of subjects, which unfold by stages and take on precise forms"[423].

## 3.3. Those Responsible

### The Priest Himself

105. The priest himself is the one primary responsible for his ongoing formation. In fact, incumbent upon each priest is

---

[423]   JOHN PAUL II, Post-Synodal Apostolic Exhortation *Pastores dabo vobis*, 79.

the duty to be faithful to the gift of God and the dynamism of daily conversion coming from the gift itself [424].

This duty stems from the fact that no one can replace the individual priest in watching over himself (cf. *1Tm* 4:16). In fact, by participating in the one priesthood of Christ, he is called to reveal and exercise, according to his unique and unrepeatable vocation, some aspect of the extraordinary richness of grace he has received.

On the other hand, the conditions and life situations of each priest are such that even from a simply human viewpoint, they demand him to be involved personally in his formation in order to capitalise on his own capabilities and possibilities.

Therefore, the priest will willingly take part in formation encounters, offering his own contributions on the basis of his skills and possibilities, and will see to it that he has and reads books and periodicals known to be of sound doctrine and proven utility for his spiritual life, and for the fruitful exercise of his ministry.

The first place among reading materials must be occupied by Sacred Scripture; followed by the writings of the Fathers, the Doctors of the Church, the ancient and modern Masters of spirituality, and by the documents of the *Magisterium* of the Church, which constitute the most authoritative and updated source of ongoing formation; the writings and the biographies of saints will also be most useful. Priests, therefore, will study and deepen them in a direct and personal manner in order to be able to present them to the lay faithful in a proper fashion.

*Fraternal Assistance*

106. Emerging in all the aspects of priestly existence are the "special bonds of apostolic charity, ministry and fraternity"[425], founded upon which is the mutual assistance priests offer one another[426]. It is to be hoped that growing and devel-

---

[424]    Cf. *ibid.*, 70.
[425]    ECUMENICAL COUNCIL VATICAN II, Decree *Presbyterorum Ordinis*, 8.
[426]    Cf. *ibid.*

oping may be cooperation among all priests in caring atten-
dance to their spiritual and human life, as well as the ministerial service. The assistance to be provided to priests in this field
can find solid support in the diverse priestly associations,
"whose statutes are recognised by the competent authority and
which, by a suitable and well tried rule of life and by fraternal
support, promote holiness in the exercise of their ministry and
foster the unity of the clergy with one another and with their
Bishop"[427].

In this perspective, respected with utmost care must be
the right of each diocesan priest to give form and substance to
his spiritual life as he best sees fit, obviously ever in conformity
with the characteristics of his vocation and the bonds stemming there from.

The work that these associations and both the Movements
and new communities approved do for priests is held in high
esteem by the Church[428], which today recognises it as a sign of
the vitality with which the Spirit never ceases in his work of
renewal.

## The Bishop

107. However large and in need of pastoral care the por-
tion of the People of God entrusted to him may be, the Bishop
must reserve very special solicitude for the ongoing formation
of his priests[429].

In fact, there is a special relationship between them and
the Bishop due to the "fact that priests receive their priesthood
from him and share his pastoral solicitude for the People of

---

[427]     *C.I.C.*, can. 278, § 2.
[428]     Cf. ECUMENICAL COUNCIL VATICAN II, Decree *Presbyterorum
Ordinis*, 8; *C.I.C.*, can. 278, § 2; JOHN PAUL II, Post-Synodal Apostolic
Exhortation *Pastores dabo vobis*, 81.
[429]     Cf. ECUMENICAL COUNCIL VATICAN II, Decree *Christus Dominus*,
16; JOHN PAUL II, Post-Synodal Apostolic Exhortation *Pastores gregis*, 47.

God"[430]. This also determines the Bishop's specific responsibility in the field of priestly formation. The Bishop must have the disposition of a father towards his priests, beginning from the seminarians, avoiding any distance or a personal style proper to a mere employer. By virtue of his function he must always be close to his priests and easily accessible. His first concern must be his priests, his collaborators in his Episcopal ministry.

Such responsibility is expressed both with respect to individual priests, whose formation must therefore be as personalised as possible, and with respect to all the priests insofar as members of the diocesan presbyterate. In this sense the Bishop will never fail to thoughtfully cultivate communication and communion among the priests, taking particular care to safeguard and promote the true character of their ongoing formation, educate their consciences to how important and necessary it is, and lastly plan and organise it by drawing up a plan of formation and providing the structures and persons to implement it[431].

In providing for the formation of his priests it is necessary for the Bishop to be involved with his own ongoing formation. Experience teaches that the more the Bishop is the first to be convinced about his own formation and engaged in it, all the better will he be able to stimulate and sustain that of his priests.

Even though his role is irreplaceable and can be delegated to no one, in this endeavour the Bishop will know how to request the collaboration of the Council of Priests, which, by virtue of its nature and aim, is the body well suited to assist him as regards, for example, the drawing up of the plan of formation.

---

[430]   JOHN PAUL II, Post-Synodal Apostolic Exhortation *Pastores dabo vobis*, 79.

[431]   Cf. *ibid.: l.c.*, 797-798.

Each Bishop will feel he is being sustained and assisted in his task by his fellow bishops in the Episcopal Conference[432].

## The Formation of Formators

108. No formation is possible without both the person who is to be formed and the person who forms, the formator. The quality and effectiveness of a plan of formation depend in part on the relative structures, but mainly on the formators.

It is evident that particularly ineluctable is the Bishop's responsibility towards these formators. First and foremost is his delicate task of forming the formators so they may have "that 'science of love' which is learned only in 'heart to heart' with Christ"[433]. Therefore, under the guidance of the Bishop these priests are to learn to harbour no other desire that to serve their confreres with this work of formation.

It is therefore necessary for the Bishop himself to appoint a "group of formators" and that the persons be chosen from among those priests highly qualified and respected for their preparation and their human, spiritual, cultural and pastoral maturity. In fact, formators must first of all be men of prayer, teachers with a strong sense of the supernatural, a profound spiritual life, exemplary conduct, with suitable experience in the priestly ministry and, like the Fathers of the Church and the holy masters of all times, able to combine spiritual requirements with the more specifically human ones of the priest. They may also be chosen from among the staff members of seminaries, centres or academic institutions approved by the ecclesiastical authority, as well as among members of religious institutes whose charism directly concerns priestly life and spirituality. Guaranteed in all cases must be the orthodoxy of doctrine and fidelity to ecclesiastical discipline. Moreover,

[432]    Cf. ECUMENICAL COUNCIL VATICAN II, Decree *Optatam totius*, 22; SACRED CONGREGATION FOR CATHOLIC EDUCATION, *Ratio Fundamentalis Institutionis Sacerdotalis* (19 March 1985), 101.
[433]    BENEDICT XVI, *Homily. Opening of the Year of Priests with the Celebration of Second Vespers* (19 June 2009): *Insegnamenti* V/1 (2009), 1036.

formators must be trusted co-workers with the Bishop, who retains ultimate responsibility for the priests, who are his most valuable collaborators.

It is also advisable to create a *planning and implementation group* separate from the group of formators to assist the Bishop is setting the topics to be considered each year as part of ongoing formation; prepare the necessary material; organise the courses, sessions, encounters and days of recollection; arrange the calendar in such as way as to foresee the absences and replacement of priests, etc. The expert advice of specialists in specific fields may also be sought.

While it would suffice to have only one group of formators, it is possible to have various planning and implementation groups if so required.

### Collaboration among Churches

109. With regard above all to collective means, the programming of the various means of ongoing formation and their concrete contents can be determined – it being understood that each Bishop retains responsibility for his own circumscription – by common agreement among various particular Churches on the national and regional level – through the respective Conferences of Bishops – as well as among adjacent dioceses or those in closer vicinity to one another. In this way, for example, used if deemed properly suited could be interdiocesan structures such as theological and pastoral faculties and institutes, as well as bodies or federations active in priestly formation. In addition to promoting authentic communion among particular Churches, this pooling of forces could offer more qualified and stimulating possibilities for ongoing formation to one and all[434].

---

[434]   Cf. JOHN PAUL II, Post-Synodal Apostolic Exhortation *Pastores dabo vobis*, 79.

*Collaboration with Academic and Spirituality Centres*

110. Furthermore, research and study institutes, centres of spirituality, as well as monasteries of exemplary observance and sanctuaries likewise constitute points of reference for theological and pastoral updating, as well as places where cultivated may be silence, adoration, the practice of confession and spiritual direction, healthy physical repose, and moments of priestly fraternity. In this manner religious families as well could collaborate in ongoing formation and contribute to that renewal of the clergy required by the new evangelisation of the Third Millennium.

## 3.4. Specific Needs Relative to Age Groups and Special Situations

*The First Years of Priesthood*

111. During the first years after Ordination priests should be helped to the utmost in finding those conditions of life and ministry that permit them to translate into practice the ideals learned during their period of formation in the seminary[435]. These first years constitute a necessary verification of their initial formation after the first delicate impact with reality, and are the most decisive ones for the future. Young priests therefore require harmonious maturation in order to be able to cope with moments of difficulty with faith and fortitude. To this end, they are to be able to benefit from the personal relationship with their Bishop and with a wise spiritual father, as well as moments of rest, meditation and monthly days of recollection. Moreover, it would seem useful to underscore the need especially for young priests to be introduced to an authentic journey of faith in the presbyterate or in the parish community, accompanied by the Bishop and by the brother priests assigned to that task.

Keeping in mind what has already been said about the pas-

---

[435]   Cf. *ibid.*, 76: *l.c.*, 793-794.

toral year, during the early years of priesthood it is necessary to organize annual formation encounters for dealing in greater depth with appropriate theological, juridical, spiritual and cultural themes, as well as special sessions dedicated to moral, pastoral and liturgical questions, etc. Such encounters may also be occasions to renew the faculty of confession as stipulated by the *Code of Canon Law* and by the Bishop[436]. It would also be useful to encourage fraternal togetherness in young priests, both among themselves and with their more mature confreres, in order to permit the exchange of experiences, mutual familiarity, and also the delicate evangelical practice of fraternal correction.

A positive experience in many places has also been the organisation, under the guidance of the Bishop, of brief encounters during the year for young priests, for example, those with less than ten years of priesthood, in order to be closer by their side while accompanying them during these early years; they will undoubtedly be occasions as well to discuss the priestly spirituality, challenges for ministers, and pastoral praxis, etc., in settings of fraternal and priestly togetherness.

Lastly, it is necessary for the young cleric to grow in a spiritual environment of true fraternity and thoughtfulness, which becomes manifest in personal attention as well for physical health and the sundry material aspects of life.

## After a Certain Number of Years

112. After a certain number of years of ministry, priests acquire solid experience and the great merit of spending themselves entirely for the spreading of the Kingdom of God in their daily work. This group of priests constitutes a great spiritual and pastoral resource.

They need encouragement, intelligent appreciation and enhancement, and a new deepening of formation in all its dimensions in order to rethink themselves and what they do; to

---

[436]    Cf. *C.I.C.*, cann. 970; 972.

reawaken the motivations underlying the sacred ministry; to do serous thinking about pastoral methods in the light of what is essential, communion among priests of the presbyterate, and friendship with the Bishop; to surmount any sense of exhaustion, frustration and solitude; to rediscover the wellsprings of the priestly spirituality[437].

It is therefore important for these priests to benefit from special and thorough formation sessions, where, in addition to theological-pastoral matters, examined would be all those psychological and emotional difficulties that may arise during that period of life. It is therefore advisable that taking part in such encounters would be not only the Bishop, but also those experts who can give a sound and valid contribution to the solution of the aforementioned problems.

*Advanced Age*

113. Elderly priests or those well along in years, who well deserve all thoughtful signs of consideration, also enter into the vital circle of ongoing formation, not so much in terms of in-depth study and cultural debate, "but rather a calm and reassuring confirmation of the part which they are still called upon to play in the Presbyterate"[438].

In addition to the formation organised for middle-aged priests, they can benefit appropriately from moments, ambits and special encounters to deepen the contemplative sense of the priestly life, rediscover and savour the doctrinal treasures of what they have already studied, and feel they are useful, as they rightly are, insofar as being of utmost value in suitable forms of true and proper ministry, especially as expert confessors and spiritual directors. In particular, they will be able to share with others their own experiences, provide encouragement, receptiveness, listening and serenity to their confreres,

---

[437]  Cf. JOHN PAUL II, Post-Synodal Apostolic Exhortation *Pastores dabo vobis*, 77.
[438]  *Ibid.*

and be available if they are summoned "to become effective teachers and trainers of other priests"[439].

*Priests in Special Situations*

114. Independently of age, priests may find themselves "in a condition of physical weakness or moral fatigue"[440]. With the offering of their sufferings they contribute in an eminent way to the work of redemption, giving "witness marked by free acceptance of the cross in the spirit of hope and Easter joy"[441].

Ongoing formation must offer these priests stimuli "to continue their service to the Church in a serene and vigorous way"[442], and to be eloquent signs of the primacy of being over doing, substance over technique, and grace over exterior efficacy. In this way they will be able to live the experience of St. Paul: "I now rejoice in my sufferings for you and in my own body to do what I can to make up all that still has to be undergone by Christ for the sake of his Church" (*Col* 1:24).

The bishop and their confreres will never fail to pay periodic visits to these their infirm brothers, who will thus be kept informed especially about events in the diocese, and thereby feel they are living members of the presbyterate and the universal Church, which they continue to edify with their suffering.

Very special and loving care must surround the priests close to concluding their days on earth spent in the service of God and for the salvation of their brothers.

The continual consolation of the faith and the prompt administration of the sacraments will be followed by the suffrages of the entire presbyterate.

---

439   *Ibid.*
440   *Ibid.*
441   *Ibid.*, 41.
442   *Ibid.*, 77.

115. At any age and in any situation a priest can experience a sense of solitude[443]. Far from being understood as psychological isolation, this can be altogether normal, a consequence of the sincere following of the Gospel, and constitute a precious dimension in his own life. In some cases, however, it could be due to special difficulties such as alienation, misunderstandings, deviations, abandonment, imprudence, limits in his own character or that of others, cases of calumny, humiliation, etc. Arising there from could be a bitter sense of frustration which would be extremely deleterious.

Nevertheless, even these moments of difficulty may become, with the help of the Lord, privileged occasions for growth along the way of holiness and the apostolate. In fact, in them the priest can discover "it is a solitude filled by the presence of the Lord"[444]. Obviously this must not make the Bishop and the entire presbyterate forget their grave responsibility in avoiding any loneliness caused by negligence with respect to priestly communion. It is incumbent upon the Diocese to decide how to hold encounters among priests so they may experience being together, learning from one another and being of assistance to one another, because no one is a priest all on his own, and exclusively in this communion with the Bishop may each priest render his service.

Nor to be forgotten are those priests who have abandoned the sacred ministry, offering them necessary help, especially through prayer and penance. The proper charitable disposition towards them, however, must not in any way lead to consider entrusting them with any ecclesiastical functions, which could create confusion and perplexity, especially among the faithful, because of their situation.

---

[443]   Cf. *ibid.,* 74.
[444]   *Ibid.*

# CONCLUSION

The Master of the harvest, who calls and sends the workers to work in is field (cf. *Mt* 9:38), has promised with eternal faithfulness: "I will give you shepherds after my own heart" (*Jr* 3:15). Resting on this divine faithfulness ever alive and at work in the Church[445] is the hope of receiving abundant and holy priestly vocations, as is already happening in many countries, as well as the certainty that the Lord will not fail to shed upon his Church the light necessary to engage in the impassioned adventure of casting the nets into the sea.

The Church responds to the gift of God with thanksgiving, fidelity, docility to the spirit, humble and insistent prayer.

In order to carry out his apostolic mission each priest will bear engraved on his heart the words of the Lord: "Father, I have glorified you on earth, having accomplished the work you gave me to do, to give eternal life to men" (*Jn* 17:2-4). For this reason he will make his own life *a gift of self* – the root and synthesis of pastoral charity – to the Church, in the likeness of the gift of Christ[446]. With joy and peace he will in this way spend his every force in helping his brothers, living as a sign of supernatural charity in obedience, celibate chastity, simplicity of life and ever respectful of the discipline in the communion of the Church.

In his work of evangelisation the priest transcends the natural order to concentrate "on things that belong to God" (*Heb* 5:1). In fact, he is called to raise man, generating him in divine life and making him grow in it unto fullness in Christ. This is why a real priest, motivated by his fidelity to Christ and to the Church, actually constitutes an incomparable force of true progress for the entire world.

---

[445]   Cf. JOHN PAUL II, Post-Synodal Apostolic Exhortation *Pastores dabo vobis*, 82.

[446]   Cf. *ibid.*, 23.

"The new evangelisation needs new evangelisers, and these are the priests who are serious about living their priesthood as a specific path toward holiness"[447]. God's works are performed by men of God!

Like Christ, the priest must present himself to the world as a model of supernatural life: "For I have given you an example, that as I have done, so you do also" (*Jn* 13:15).

The witness given by life itself qualifies the priest and constitutes his most convincing preaching. Ecclesiastical discipline itself, lived with genuine interior motivation, proves to be providential help for living his own identity, fostering charity, and bringing light to bear on that witness without which any cultural preparation or strict programming would be naught but illusory. *Doing* serves no purpose if there is no *being with Christ*.

Here lies the horizon of the identity, life, ministry and ongoing formation of the priest: a task of immense work that is open, courageous, enlightened by the faith, sustained by hope and rooted in charity.

No one is alone in this work, which as necessary as it is urgent. It is necessary for priests to be helped through exemplary, authoritative and resolute action of pastoral governance exercised by their respective Bishops in transparent communion with the Apostolic See, as well as by the fraternal collaboration of the presbyterate at large, and the entire people of God.

Each priest is to entrust himself to Mary, the Star of the new evangelisation. She "has been a model of that motherly love with which all who join in the Church's apostolic mission for the regeneration of mankind should be animated"[448], and priests will find in her constant protection and assistance for the renewal of their lives and for helping their priesthood give rise to a more intense and renewed thrust of evangelisation in this third millennium of Redemption.

---

[447]   *Ibid.*, 82.
[448]   ECUMENICAL COUNCIL VATICAN II, Dogmatic Constitution *Lumen gentium*, 65.

*The Supreme Pontiff, Benedict XVI, on 14 January 2013, approved this Directory and ordered its publication.*

Rome, from the *Palazzo delle Congregazioni*, this 11 day of February in the year 2013, the memoria of Our Lady of Lourdes.

MAURO Card. PIACENZA
*Prefect*

✠ CELSO MORGA IRUZUBIETA
*Titular Archbishop of Alba marittima*
*Secretary*

# Prayer to Mary Most Holy

Oh Mary,
Mother of Jesus Christ and Mother of priests,
accept this title which we bestow on you
to celebrate your motherhood
and to contemplate with you the priesthood
of your Son and of your sons,
oh holy Mother of God.

Oh Mother of Christ,
to the Messiah - priest you gave a body of flesh
through the anointing of the Holy Spirit
for the salvation of the poor and the contrite of heart;
guard priests in your heart and in the Church,
oh Mother of the Saviour.

Oh Mother of Faith,
you accompanied to the Temple the Son of Man,
the fulfilment of the promises given to the fathers;
give to the Father for his glory
the priests of your Son,
oh Ark of the Covenant.

Oh Mother of the Church,
in the midst of the disciples in the upper room
you prayed to the Spirit
for the new people and their shepherds;
obtain for the Order of Presbyters
a full measure of gifts,
oh Queen of the Apostles.

Oh Mother of Jesus Christ,
you were with him at the beginning
of his life and mission,
you sought the Master among the crowd,
you stood beside him when he was lifted
up from the earth
consumed as the one eternal sacrifice,

and you had John, your son, near at hand;
accept from the beginning those
who have been called,
protect their growth,
in their life ministry accompany
your sons,
oh Mother of Priests.

Amen[449].

---

[449]    JOHN PAUL II, Post-Synodal Apostolic Exhortation *Pastores dabo vobis*, 82.

# INDEX

TIPOGRAFIA  VATICANA